Baghdad to Bombay

In the Kitchens of My Cousins

Pearl Sofaer

Paper Jam Publishing
Post Office Box 435 • Eastsound, WA 98245
Design and Production by Eileen Dean and Lin McNulty

Library of Congress Control Number: 2008924536

Sofaer, Pearl
Baghdad to Bombay: In the Kitchens of My Cousins

First printing, March 2008
ISBN: 978-1-888345-24-7
Printed in the United States

10 9 8 7 6 5 4 3 2 1

For My Children

Baghdad to Bombany

Table of Contents

ℭ *Acknowledgments*

Thank you to my fellowship of family and friends. Their trust and encouragement helped me immeasurably in the creation of this book. In particular, Aunt Girlie, Uncle Sass, and Uncle Joe, my brothers Abe and Ike, and numerous cousins generously shared their stories and recipes. Many of my cousins live in Israel, Australia, and New Zealand, so thanks to Marian for helping me visit these places to do my reporting.

The ad hoc team of editors who slashed, burned, and gave me constructive criticism included Abby, Daniel, Edmund, Gail, Genevieve, Lisa, Michael Meka–Deva, and Pat. Thank you for helping to shape the book. Their devoted work was followed up by Roslyn Schloss, who edited the final manuscript. And cheers to Eileen and Lin, who took the manuscript and turned it into a book.

Craig Sherod brought my collection of photos to life, making them look fresh without losing their historic patina, then painstakingly placing them throughout the book. My friend Jan Wolski began and completed the initial manuscript with me, performed countless computer tasks, edited, listened, and offered a great many positive suggestions. Finally, my son, Ben, was always there with ideas for layouts, edits, and answers to the million questions I had for him. Thanks to you all.

Throughout the years I have kept no diary or journal, so it's possible that my memory has sometimes fooled me. If so, please forgive me.

Pearl Sofaer, 2008

ℭ *Author's Note*

I am standing in front of a large old wooden cupboard. The knotholes and network of deep cracks resemble the fabric of my favorite pair of jeans. It reminds me of the almirah (cupboard) that was part of my parents' first set of furniture. The center, a large open space spanned by weathered shelves, is framed by two narrow doors on either side. The side doors are open and I reach in and pull out handfuls of gold coins, paper money and rich colorful bolts of cloth. They spill into my arms and I am smiling.

I had this dream while I was going through my divorce, struggling to cope with the financial and emotional turmoil that was the residue of 20 years of marriage. I slept well that night and can still remember waking up refreshed, with a smile on my face. The dream felt like an important turning point, but I had no idea what it meant. I related it to my parents and my father looked thrilled. As my story unfolded, his face broke into an even wider smile. "You see, Pearl," he said, " the riches of your family have been placed in your hands. Perhaps you will do something with this wealth someday."

Thirty years later the wealth of my family is strewn across my desk. It's all here: the small, private stories; the joys and tragedies of the precious people I grew up with; the added gifts of those who joined, or were born into, our clan. This book collects many of the stories of our beloved family, the celebrations and the unforgettable feasts I shared with my cousins in beautiful Bombay.

CR *Introduction*

M y cousins and I learned the art of hospitality at an early age. We inherited the custom of welcoming people into our homes from the historical cultures of the Middle East and India and through the Jewish tradition. When friends or family arrive in Sydney, the Moses David clan is ready and waiting with feasts of Indian curries, barbecued Australian meats and *hameems*, the traditional Sabbath dish. In Jerusalem, the lavish table at Alice and Effry Jonah's home combines the spices and tastes of Baghdad, Calcutta and Czechoslovakia, all served with the warmth and love that permeates this terrace flat. And in Montreal, Joyce and Norman Hecht, former competitors in the Maccabiah, Israel's Olympics, are ready to eat, drink and dance with their visiting cousins.

None of us have adopted the system in India where the host must insist that a guest eat more. The guest will usually answer, "Oh no. Thank you. I just couldn't." The host will implore the guest to have more of something else. Again, the guest will make excuses and say, "Oh no, thank you." The host will then invite the guest to partake of some other delicacy. After this third gesture by the host, it is protocol for the guest to politely reply, "Very well. If you insist. But really, you are being too good to me." My families of the Ezekiel and Sofaer clans like to eat too much and have historically bypassed this delightful repartee.

In Bombay, my late cousin Lulu Patel would ask, "What do you want to eat?" and my first answer was always "fried pomfret," which prompted Rajab, her cook, to go off to the beach and return with fresh caught Bay of Bengal fish neatly wrapped in newspaper. Lulu never cooked. She seemed to have a difficult time even making cheese sandwiches, which she loved. But her small flat and big heart welcomed the world. Cousins and friends and friends of friends, from every part of the globe visited Lulu in Bombay. Her kitchen was constantly humming and the floors in the flat were often covered with mattresses.

Arriving once in London in the middle of the night en route from Bombay to New York, I stayed with my cousin Fred Ezekiel and his wife, Nina. At that late hour, completely exhausted and famished, I was treated to a heartwarming *shorbah* (chicken and rice soup) made by Nina, in her inimitable Baghdadi way. That's the only way to go to sleep after a long tiring flight. It made me feel like a little girl being tucked into bed for soft and sweet dreams and reminded me of *pish pash*, a soup that we were given when we were sick. And on a trip to Sydney, my cousin Susanna Sofaer surprised me with a *congee*, the Chinese version of *shorbah*. Or, who knows, in Iraq we may have copied the Chinese. Both are nourishing and delicious.

Besides our DNA, we have one major commonality: our enthusiasm for food. We have incorporated a variety of cuisine into our traditions, including the obvious British, American and Australian, but also Chinese, Czechoslovakian, Indian, Iraqi and German. No longer do we have *marag* (Iraqi chicken soup) at least three times a week. There is much more to taste and enjoy.

Many of my cousins grew up in hardship. Perhaps as a result of their difficult lives they were eager and ambitious to work for their gracious homes and financial independence. They learned quickly to make the most of every opportunity. With family as the core of their existence, my cousins are an inspiration for this book and to everyone they meet. I have traveled four continents to speak with as many of my first and second cousins as possible. Thanks to their openness, I can now share their passion and stories handed down to us by our forefathers from Babylon, Baghdad and Bombay. I invite you to come into the kitchens of my cousins to share their favorite meals and enjoy a vital tapestry of our history and personal reminiscences.

Baghdad to Bombay

In the Kitchens of My Cousins

Beginnings

Part I

❧ *From Baghdad to Bombay*

Our story begins in Babylon and Baghdad, located between the Tigris and Euphrates rivers, and known as Mesopotamia. These cities of my heritage always prompt me to wonder what life was like in the time of my ancestors. Were the streets paved with packed-down mud clay after centuries of time? Would I have covered my face as I did in India because of the dust everywhere? What were the homes like? In archaeological digs in Israel, large boulders made of clay and sometimes rocks themselves, seem to have been the preferred building materials in the early centuries A.D., so I assume Babylon may have been similar. With pictures of Baghdad currently in the news, we see a more modern city that is reminiscent of Bombay.

Aden 1948 – synagogue destroyed

And what about the Jewish people? Did they live within a designated part of Baghdad like the city of Aden on the Southern Arabian peninsula? In Aden I saw two streets of "Jewish" homes. A bombed-out synagogue and a Jewish school stood as bookends of this tiny neighborhood.

I have tried to imagine being a Jewish woman in old Baghdad. Would I have been a second-class citizen or would I have been encouraged to attend school? How did people dress? Perhaps much the same as my uncle Ezra and aunt Chichani did in Bombay. Auntie Chichani wore laapars (the Middle Eastern equivalent of the Hawaiian muumuu) while Uncle Ezra wore the loose and comfortable pants and long shirt of the Middle East, along with a fez. Many people dressed in Western style, but white cottons seemed more practical in the desert climate.

Our forefathers were brought to Babylon, in approximately 597 BCE. Nebuchadnezzar, king of Persia, took the leading and most useful citizens of Judah back to Babylon as slaves:

> He carried them into exile all Jerusalem: all the officers and the fighting men and all the craftsmen and artisans – a total of ten thousand. Only the poorest people of the land were left. (2 Kings 24:14)

Later he returned to Judah, destroyed the Temple of Solomon and massacred most of the inhabitants of the city.

The Jews lived in Babylon and then Baghdad for more than 2,600 years. They toiled in a rich and fertile valley, where the fruit and flowers had memorable tastes, scents and color. They were eventually freed from slavery and accepted as free citizens, becoming important traders in the Mediterranean basin. Distinguished scholars created the Talmud (Judaic law) while scribes wrote down the Torah (the five books of Moses) for the first time. Abraham of Ur, known as the father of Judaism, introduced the Mesopotamian Jews to the belief in one God. Ideas spread across the Mediterranean to Jewish scholars in Spain and Egypt and the tenets of Judaism were continually shared between these teachers and their students. Imagine communicating across these distances without phones or computers, instead waiting for a ship and then a caravan rider to bring answers to a question or to present debating points for argument.

My maternal grandfather's family was known as Hanassi ye Haskell Bechor in Persia. Their large clan, referred to as "a thousand strong," had business dealings with the sultan of Persia. They bought and sold all the sultan's crops and although they were highly respected among traders, their wealth and sizable share of trade eventually created a feud between them and the sultan. After an unknown number of years in Persia, they moved to Kirkuk, then a part of Turkey and now a city in Iraq.

All my great-grandparents were born in Iraq and were traders between Iraq and major Mediterranean cities. In the late 1800s and early 1900s, some of them moved to India and Burma to expand their businesses and participate in the expansion of trade created by the East India Company. Both in India and in Burma, Jews were treated with respect, had no experience of anti-Semitism and were free to create peaceful and successful lives.

Throughout their 2,600 year stay in Mesopotamia, now known as Iraq, Jews were victims of numerous *farhuds* (pogroms). With the declaration of the State of Israel in 1948, life for a Jew in Iraq became untenable. Over 110,000 Jews left Iraq and approximately 10,000 Jews left Iran between 1948 and 1952 to settle in Israel. In spite of the harsh circumstances in Iraq, it was painful for Iraqi Jews to leave their homes. They had immersed themselves in the culture of Iraq, much like the Jews in Europe who had known their homelands for centuries and were distraught at leaving in the years leading up to the Second World War. Today, hints of Iraq are echoed in our names, our foods are Iraqi, and most of our elders still speak Arabic. Our old prayer books were written in Hebrew but read in Arabic and Aramaic.

The Baghdadi Jews in Bombay were a community of over 20,000 when my family lived there. Yet, they knew everything there was to know about one another. They knew the name of a person's grandmother; where she came from, her family history — was the family rich; were there health or mental problems in the line; was the family respectable. It went on and on. I feel fortunate to know so much about who we are, where we came from and the authenticity of our background for so many centuries. Our children and their children now in other lands are losing this knowledge abruptly because they are not part of a village like I was in Bombay. A village where it was common to hear: "Oh, you mean Menashe. He was the son of Isaac the shoemaker, who lived in Basra. He moved to Baghdad to marry Esther. She was from Tehran. Their son, Haskell, lives in Tel Aviv now with six children and eight grandchildren. Haskell's wife, Masooda, came from Cairo."

Listening to such an exchange, my cousins and I would giggle and look wide-eyed at one another. We knew where we came from because our parents and our aunts and uncles gossiped, or so it seemed. My mother's father told her that they were of the tribe of "Benjamin." That would be difficult to prove, but the verbal information was passed on from generation to generation, so who knows? It is my hope that "Baghdad to Bombay" will evoke curiosity and questioning in its readers and that they will become the chroniclers of their own generation and the generations to come.

My mother told me stories about her father's mother, who had lived in Isfahan. Isfahan has been described as the most beautiful city of Persia (now Iran) and I imagine a place of broad avenues, beautiful buildings, and many, many gardens with flowers, birds, and the sound of flowing water. I picture gardens like the Hanging Gardens on top of Malabar Hill in Bombay, with topiaries of animals in the Bombay zoo lining the paths through scores of flower beds. And I hear the sounds of the waterfalls among flowering bushes and trees like the Bund Gardens in Poona. It must have been wonderful to grow up in Isfahan.

When Great-grandmother married, she lived in a primitive farmhouse in Kirkuk where goats and chickens ran through the house, according to my mother. My great-grandmother was a very short woman who wore a shirt with a vest, pants tucked into boots, and a scarf around her head. She always had two rifles strapped around her chest to safeguard herself and her many children from the marauders of western Iraq and the Steppes of Russia. Sad tales of young girls who were carried away by marauders have been part of our family history and our great-grandmother, tiny as she was, had the fearlessness of a Kurd, ready to protect and attack those who dared to extinguish the lights of her lineage. We are all proud bearers of the strength and adaptability we have inherited from the Kurds.

Following the Iraqi custom of identifying people by their place of birth, my mother's father Ephraim, was known as "Ephraim Kirkuklie." His family spoke Aramaic, Arabic, Farsi, and Turkish, and he grew up on family land in the midst of the richest oilfields of Kirkuk. As he told my mother, "If you put your hand in the ground, it came out black."

After moving to Bombay, Grandfather Ephraim went back to Kirkuk to bring his father to India. Great-grandfather Haskell begged his son not to take him away from his home, saying "You are taking me to my death." Haskell said he knew he would die on the ship and begged to be left alone. His son carried him onto the ship by force and, unhappily, Haskell's intuition proved right. He was buried at sea somewhere between Basra and Bombay.

In Bombay the Ezekiels, my mother's family, became known for their particular form of *habra* (welfare). They wanted a thriving Jewish community in Bombay and conducted many searches for good Jewish women from Baghdad to travel to India and become wives for the newly arrived Jewish bachelors. They paid all the costs of travel, dowries and homes, and helped the couples establish themselves with work and decent incomes. For this reason the brothers Ezekiel - Benjamin, Ephraim, Ezra and Menasseh - were much loved in Bombay.

Great-grandmother Aziza Smouha Mitana　　*Great-grandfather Shaoul Mitana*

My maternal grandmother, Lulu Mitana, was born in Baghdad and educated in Arabic and French like most Jewish girls in Baghdad.

She and her large family moved to Bombay with her parents, Aziza and Shaul Mitana, after Shaul established lines of business between Baghdad, Bombay and Alexandria. Lulu met Ephraim in Bombay and they married some time after his first wife, Simha, died. I was named after Grandmother Lulu (Arabic for Pearl), as were seven of my cousins. Both my parents were one of ten siblings. We had twenty aunts and uncles and were originally a total of 56 first cousins.

Lulu and Ephraim Ezekiel with their eldest child, Victoria

My paternal grandparents, Meyer Sofaer and Hannah David, were born in Burma in the late 1800s. Granny was born in Rangoon, where the David family had settled years before. She was not educated formally and spoke only Arabic and Hindi. Grandpa was born on the Irrawadi River as his family approached their new home on the long journey from Baghdad. What a brave woman my grandfather's mother must have been. Imagine being pregnant, with a small son and traveling from Baghdad to Burma in the late 1880s. Not an easy journey even today. And then stopping in a small, unknown village, in an unknown land, to give birth to her second son.

Grandpa and Granny in Rangoon

Hannah was only 13 and Meyer was 19 when they married. She was petite, under five feet tall, and had never attended school. He was medium height and handsome, well educated and sophisticated. It has always amazed me that their marriage was a match made in heaven.

Grandpa became a wealthy man in Rangoon. He represented Del Monte and Hunt's, and imported whiskeys, wines and specialty foods from around the world that he sold throughout Southeast Asia from his *godowns* (warehouses) on the docks of Rangoon. He told me once that his favorite cities in the world were Paris and Oakland, California, where he was wined and dined by the Del Monte family. In the early 1900s both cities had broad avenues and many parks, and traffic moved around circles of small gardens. Grandpa loved to travel and shared his passion with his family, taking them to Kyoto and Peking during the hot summer months. I remember two tall Ming vases in his flat in Bombay, which he brought back from one of these holidays.

When my father, my sister-in-law Marian and I visited Rangoon in 1984, we went to the Musmeah Yeshua synagogue my dad had attended as a boy. We were able to look at a large ledger of births that was kept in the synagogue and it was wonderful to see all the names of my aunts and uncles. Then we made a rather amusing discovery. Dad had always told us his birthday was May 15th. Yet here it was: May 14th, the same day as my sister Shoshanna. I remembered how upset he had been when Shoshanna was born on the 14th instead of the 15th like him. He had turned to my mother and said, "Couldn't you wait one more day?" Well, she had it right and we telephoned her from Burma to tell her. Dad, on the other hand, refused to accept his actual birth date. His response was, "My birthday has always been May 15th and that's what it will remain."

Dad on the Sofaer bench, Burma Synagogue

The building and grounds are now encircled by a wall of shops, the rent from which is used to maintain the synagogue, the graveyard, and the compound. Only a handful of Jews remain in Rangoon now and most of the synagogue's visitors are Jews from abroad. The interior is very simple with rows of hard wooden benches for worshipers. Unfortunately, the graveyard has been robbed and most of the marble gravestones are broken or stolen.

As Dad and I entered the synagogue, he took my hand and led me to the benches that were used by the Sofaer family. "Now you are seated with the rest of the family," he said. As we sat together, the clock in the room began to chime and Dad quietly began to cry. He told me that the sound of the chimes had taken him back more than 70 years. It was the same clock that he remembered as a boy. "Everything is so very different from what I remember. This has been hard on me," he said. Sometimes, you can't go home again.

In Bombay we grew up in a Technicolor world: beautiful Indian women in their saris of brilliant red, purple, green, orange, blue and yellow, often sprinkled with silver and gold; the Banjara Hills gypsies in their multicolored skirts and *cholis* (short blouses) hand-embroidered with pieces of glass; the red-turbaned men of Rajasthan, their heads towering above the crowd; and even the cars and animal carts, decorated in colors unseen in the West. Once, years later, as I waited at Heathrow for my plane after a month in India, I began to feel choked and sad. I realized there were no colors around me. Everyone was wearing bland gray, black, brown or beige.

The sounds in Bombay were reminiscent of a Genghis Khan invasion, full of clamor, and high passion. Like the passion for our heritage and love of our tradition. The passion for singing in Arabic, English, Hebrew, and Hindi and dancing to swing, to tangos and to the beat of Um Kulthum. We danced on Juhu Beach, on the street near our synagogue, or on the terrace above a temple to the sounds of the temple drums.

We love to travel, we love to eat and most of all, we are passionate about one another. Why be involved if not totally involved? Why cook for two when you could easily invite ten? Every part of our lives is ratcheted up and we feel energized rather than depleted. We have integrated into the many cultures of our new homelands and have expanded our global experience to create our own miniature United Nations. We have learned new languages, new dress and behavior codes, new slang and new ways of looking at the rest of the world. We have become Aussies and Londoners; and in Israel we call our children *sabras*. We speak fluent Hebrew, and Hindi, with an American accent. We are a huge surprise to one another in all our differences.

߷ *Our Baghdad Family*

I didn't know I had family still living in Baghdad until 1941, when my mother's brother David's wife, Aunt Naima, arrived at our flat in Bombay with my five cousins. A *farhud* (pogrom) had been declared in Iraq and, since Uncle David held a British passport, she and their children were evacuated by the British to Bombay. Aunt Naima and my cousins Clairette, Fred, May, Floty, and Shoullie stayed in Bombay for nine months before returning to Baghdad. Uncle David, remained in Baghdad, where the British Legation became the safe compound for British subjects.

Rashid Ali El Kaylani, the ruler of Iraq, had declared the *farhud* against the Jews. Together with the Grand Mufti of Jerusalem, he applied Nazi tactics across the Middle East that resulted in the deaths over the course of three days, of more than 150 Jewish men, women, and children in Baghdad. A family friend, Aaron, who was born in Baghdad and lived there in 1941, shared a story about a Muslim friend. The Muslim friend came to Aaron's house and took all of Aaron's family to his home. He then set up a guard outside and told his Muslim neighbors, "You will have to kill me and all my children before you can touch one hair on their heads."

As soon as Aunt Naima and her children arrived in Bombay, she went to Aunt Chichani who dismissed them angrily. Chichani was convinced that Uncle David had stolen her husband Ezra's wealth in Iraq. My mother told me that she and other family members, signed an agreement drafted by Uncle Ezra to sell the oil rich family land in Kirkuk to a British oil company. Fred, my mother's brother Jacob's son, says that his father tore up the papers when he saw that the land's resources had been described as "agriculture" and not "oil." Jacob knew that the British would pay a great deal less for "agriculture."

Uncle Ezra set off for Kirkuk with his servant Babu without any signatures for a sale, confident he would bring back money for the entire family. When he got there he had to chase squatters off the land and began putting the property into order for the sale. Unfortunately, he had a "wandering eye," and quickly became enchanted with two young girls ages 15 and 17, both of whom he promptly married. He was certainly no youngster, but it was acceptable in Kirkuk for an older man to marry a much younger woman, and often more than one at a time. His diversion cost him his life and the family their rich inheritance. He was shot to death in bed by some of the squatters; Babu, who was also shot, was seriously injured. The British took over the land and the family received nothing. Chichani's grief over her husband's loss made her shut her door on anyone who reminded her of Baghdad.

Uncle Ezra and his hookah with nephew, Orie Ezra

Shocked by Chichani's anger, Naima went with the children to the home of my mother's brother Aman before coming to our flat. My world became larger with the arrival of cousins. The pillow fights, the playing in the park and then introducing them to our Bombay way of life were great fun for me. But how we all managed in our two-bedroom flat has flown from my memory. I remember how much I missed them when they moved into their own flat in Byculla, at least half-an-hour from our home by car where they attended the Jewish school with our other cousins.

After nine months when they returned by ship to Baghdad, Uncle Jacob insisted that they eat only kosher food on the voyage and supplied them with a huge bag of bananas, a barrel of mango pickle and sardines. My cousin Fred has since said, "We ate nothing but sardines for a whole week and it was 35 years before I could put a sardine in my mouth."

Simha, mother of David, Jack, Aman,
Jacob and Rebecca – Baghdad

The perspective of my Baghdad cousins on the Middle East, Judaism, and the world, is broader than mine. They experienced anti-Semitism first-hand in Iraq during World War II. At the same time, they were nourished by centuries of knowledge in the land of

Mesopotamia, the birthplace of the Hebrew alphabet and the Talmud. To quote my cousin May, "Life in Baghdad was deceptively idyllic—a child oriented society on the one hand, but harsh on the other, with public executions commonplace." Fred feels it taught them to "depend on yourself...and when your back is to the wall you have to fight, you have to work, you have no time to horse around." Basically, he says, "you have no time to scratch your head."

My cousins were immersed in their religious heritage. In Baghdad they attended a Jewish School, the Alliance Israelite, where they learned French and English. They spoke French at school but also knew three Arabic dialects: one for the Arabs, one for the Christians, and one for the Jews. As Jews they were considered third-class citizens and had to use the correct dialect when they spoke to a Muslim, a Christian or a Jew. This kept them out of trouble with their neighbors and sharpened their ears when they learned more languages. Prayers in Hebrew were taught at home by a teacher to the children as we did in Bombay. But the Iraq government passed laws that limited minorities to learning just their prayers and not the spoken Hebrew because, as Fred put it, "they were afraid that every minority would have it's own language and then there would be a 'Tower of Babble.'"

The Jews of Baghdad dressed like Europeans except when they went to the *suk* (the Arab market) where mothers wore the black *abaya*, a full-length dress that totally covers a woman. Not only did this form of dress keep a woman safe in the market, it kept the identity of a savvy bargainer well hidden. The Jewish men, whether in European suits or Arab dress, often wore fezzes like the ones my grandfather Ephraim produced and sold to the Arabs. But Uncle David always wore European suits and ties and was proud that he was a British subject.

As children my cousins were involved in sports, much like we were in Bombay, but only within their community of Jews. Sometimes Uncle David hired a boat and they were taken to play and swim on an island in the Tigris River. The boatsman would catch carp, known as "river fish" in Baghdad and barbecue the catch for their dinner, which Naima enhanced with fresh fruit and vegetables. [Since the bombings in Iraq during the first Gulf War these fish have almost disappeared.] They would return home in an *arabana*, a horse-drawn carriage, but the final steps through the narrow lanes had to be made on foot.

They played the famous Middle Eastern game *towli* (backgammon) and turned their dining room table into an adequate Ping-Pong table. Their parents were way ahead of their time in developing the creativity of their children and allowed them to paint, draw, or write on one large wall that was whitewashed annually. Other special events were the outdoor movies where they sat on the grass in a park in front of a large screen enjoying the latest that both Hollywood and Bollywood had to offer.

Aunt Naima grew up in a large house with many of her relatives. Her grandparents, their children, and their children's children lived together and shared the family wealth and responsibilities. In Iraq this type of home is known as "The Big House." They had a communal system within the house and each member participated in the daily chores and activities to the best of their ability. It served as security for each of them when they were older or in need of help. When Naima married she moved into a small house she had inherited from her father, in the Christian quarter near Rashid Street (homes descended matrilineally in the Jewish community in Iraq). All the lanes were of mud and during the winter you were lucky to have boots. The red-brick floors of the bedrooms were covered with Persian carpets during the winter. The children played in a roofless open courtyard laid with 10-inch-square yellow bricks and off the courtyard were one large common room and two bedrooms.

Aden – beds on rooftops

Everyone in the family slept on the roofs over the two bedrooms on the hot summer nights. My cousin May, who remembers these nights as magical, wondered why only her parents had white curtains draped around their four-poster bed but she didn't ask. The fun of sleeping under the stars included playing with the children on the neighboring roofs, throwing balls to one another and competing with flying kites. Occasionally, the dreaded sand storms came to Baghdad and battered everything in their path. Most families spent those days and nights in the kitchen cellars, reluctantly leaving the magic of the night skies.

My cousins' home was quite primitive with a small ice box in the kitchen, just one bathroom with a shower and a faucet with cold running water in the basement. The kitchen had no counters so Naima had to crouch on the concrete floor, as we did in India, to prepare all meals. Bathing took place in the bathroom and Naima carried buckets of hot water upstairs to bathe the children. My cousin Floty recalls that her mother bathed her until they left for England when Floty was 10. To offset all her hard work, Naima had a helper who washed the clothes, cleaned the house, and sometimes shopped for her in the market.

They kept a kosher kitchen and May recollects baking *matzoh* in a five-foot-high wood-burning mud oven, called a *tenour*. Preparations took days and included Jewish friends and neighbors kneading and rolling out large round pita style bread that baked in a few minutes. The women worked hard but happily, content in their commitment to the ritual of unleavened bread during Passover week and enjoying the camaraderie of one another's company.

Their lives were as narrow as the lanes in their quarter, where they had either to walk or to have a donkey carry their loads of watermelons or bushel bags of tomatoes to their home. Naima would cook the tomatoes, grind and strain them, then leave the juice on trays on the roof in the sun. As the sun evaporated the juice, they were able to store as many as six trays of tomato paste from an original ten and these were packed and kept in the basement to use during the winter. A cow was brought to the house every day and was milked in front of someone in the family to make sure that water was not added. My cousins could never go beyond their limited circle of family and Jewish friends while the men could have contact with other men "from the outside," Muslims or Christians with whom they did business, but never were involved with them socially. The children's isolation led to a lack of close connection between them and the older male relatives. (It was the same in India, where "children were to be seen, not heard.")

The Jews of Baghdad, like those in Bombay, held the male children in higher esteem than the girls. A girl in Bombay was only worth a dowry if she was "fair" enough to be considered a beauty, one who could attract a "good catch"—a boy from a well-respected and rich family who had an education. As cousin Floty puts it, "A boy was a pleasure, a girl was a curse." Sometimes the pressures were too much for a girl. May recalls a story her mother once told her: When Naima found herself in the same shop as her fiancee, she promptly fainted as that was the best way out. Naima had a *shidduch*, or arranged marriage, which set strict codes of behavior for both parties. Foremost among these rules was that the couple could not be seen together in public, lest they fuel speculation that they were having a premarital affair. Suspicion and gossip permeated the Baghdad way of life.

There are many versions of this story. According to both Floty and Uncle Jack, David's brother, the marriage was not arranged. Jack's story was that they met, fell in love and got married. If David and Naima did indeed choose each other as mates, this rarely occurred in the Iraq of their time and would have given the gossipmongers a lot to talk about. Shoullie insists he knows the correct story directly from his mother. He says that prior to David's arrival in Baghdad, Naima had refused to accept an offer of marriage, unheard of in Baghdad, and walked out of a meeting with her future husband because she did not like him. May concurs and said there was no chance anyone else would have made another offer after that. David went to the *dalal* (matchmaker), who fixed him up with Naima. They met and David asked her, "Can you cook? Can you sew? Can you care for me and our children?" Naima asked no questions. She told Shoullie, "I looked at him. He had two eyes, two arms and two legs. He wasn't bald, he spoke English and he was a British subject." (Who could ask for anything more?) Shoullie backs up his story with, "Their marriage was definitely arranged because when Dad got mad at my mother, he swore at the matchmaker." Floty disagrees with Shoullie and said that when David came to Baghdad, "he met my mother and fell in love with her and settled there and stayed there."

Uncle David, Aunt Naima holding Fred, Clairette
and Aunt Naima's sister, Regina

In Iraq limits were placed on the family's fortunes and potential. A Jew could be a merchant or a goldsmith but rarely would he have a job in government, the schools, the police, or other civil servant positions. Fred said it best in a letter dated "Baghdad 21st September, 1946" sent to Uncle Joe, Uncle David's brother, who was then in New York:

"Dear, I hope that you appreciate full well how a foreigner with such a Faith seeking a living is treated in such a country, especially if he is poor. He is spurned, mocked and trod underfoot. There is no chance to prosper, no way to improve, no help to rise, not the faintest hope of success and not the slightest expectation of getting a good job. There is no appreciation for his works, no praise for his deeds and no encouragement for his attempts. Once he leaves his school then there is for him nothing for anything. He is condemned to spend his days in idleness and to beg his living."

Fred excelled in the sciences and was accepted to MIT, where he became a professor after graduation. He eventually founded a company with a patent of his own after having consulted and created patents for other companies. His son David has now taken over the business and Fred calls himself the CPO, the "chief packaging officer." Behind him throughout the years, quiet and constant, has been his beautiful wife, Bessie, whom Fred describes as "a real gem." He was so very shy that when he proposed to Bessie he said, "Do you think your parents would like me as a son-in-law?" And she said, "Yes." Then they went home and announced that they were engaged. I was one of the lucky ones to attend their beautiful wedding at the MIT chapel and hear the sweet words of Kahlil Gibran quoted at the ceremony. America was a good choice for Shoullie too, who also became an esteemed professor at MIT.

In 1948, with the emergence of the state of Israel in an unfriendly Middle East, the British urged Uncle David to leave Baghdad with his family. They could stay in Iraq, but they could no longer enjoy protection as British subjects. David decided to leave with his family after the children were trapped and locked in their school overnight. Luckily for them, his longtime British employers, Frank C. Strick & Co, gave them one-way airline passage to England. The Ezekiels of Baghdad soon became the Ezekiels of London. (They have since evolved into the Ezekiels of Australia, Boston and Toronto.)

For both Uncle David and Aunt Naima the leave taking was bittersweet. Baghdad was their beloved home in spite of the dangers that loomed around them. But these were known dangers. Now they were forced to face the unknown in London. They did not even know where they would stay when they arrived in London. Floty recalled, "I certainly remember that night. It was raining and dark. The cab driver was overwhelmed by all of us and said, 'Where?' When we answered 'take us where you wish,' he said, in shock, '*Blymie*...you have nowhere to go. How did you get here? ' He went to many hotels and a lot of them were full (or they did not want to take us in). We finally ended up in Euston, very close to the Euston tube station." They found a home that was run by a kindly couple and felt somewhat reassured.

Fortunately they were able to sell their place in Baghdad and used the 3,000 pounds as a down payment on a very small house in Hendon that remained their home until they headed to Australia in 1959. A few months after they left Baghdad other Jews were told that they could stay and be loyal Iraqi citizens or leave with only $100, one suitcase, and the clothes on their backs. The Jews who left were forced to give the keys to their homes to a policeman and say, "This is your house; not mine anymore."

Although life was strange and difficult in England, there was a sense of relief. In England, they would not be put out of their homes, murdered, or hung. They slept without fear for the first time in years. "No longer did people throw stones or spit at us because we were Jews," said Floty. At the same time, they did not seem to be Jews to their Ashkenazi neighbors, who did not understand the sounds of the Baghdad Hebrew. Their being Mizrachi set them apart from the mainstream of Jews in England and created more isolation for them. In England they felt lost because nothing was familiar in their daily and social routines.

Cooking without spices like cumin, cardamom, and turmeric became a challenge for Naima. She made *hameem*, or *t'bith*, as some call it in Iraq, and always cooked it with eggs, which she put on a pan on top of the rice and chicken before covering the entire pot. There could be no Sabbath, of course, without *hameem*, a dish that originated in Iraq and is cooked every Friday before sundown. In Bombay, where most homes didn't have ovens in the 1940s and early 1950s, we cooked it on a *sigree*, a barbecue on the floor fuelled with hot charcoal. The pot was then covered with gunny sacks to cook all night and the *hameem* was eaten for lunch on Saturday when we returned from synagogue. With generous leftovers from Friday night's dinner, we never had to cook on the Sabbath.

Clairette, the eldest of Naima and David's children, loves *bamya* or okra and uses it in an Iraqi recipe with chicken, fresh tomatoes and spices. Okra was a popular vegetable in their home and Naima dried countless lines of threaded *bamya* in the sun to use during the winters in Iraq. Since *bamya* was supposed to be an aphrodisiac, it was always served at Friday night dinner in fulfillment of the *mitzvah* commanding that a husband must sleep with his wife on Sabbath and satisfy her. The obligation, of course, went both ways, and no *eshet hayil* (virtuous woman) could have a headache on Sabbath eve.

Bernie Friedman was working in London when he met, fell in love with, and married beautiful Clairette. He was born in Sydney. Clairette was born in Baghdad. Two people from very different cultures got together and created a successful love affair, partnership, and wonderful family in Australia. Bernie's grandparents Emma and Jacob Glass had separately emigrated to England from their native Poland between 1879 and 1881. They met in London, married, and headed to Australia, a country that welcomed enterprise and hard work. Australia was no longer just a place for convicts whom the British government shipped to the "Rocks." Indeed, the Glass family prospered with the offspring of Emma and Jacob growing to 150 descendants in their chosen homeland. That's a long way from the *shtetls* of Poland.

Floty, Shoullie, May, Bernie and Clairette (standing) - London
Aunt Naima, Uncle David and Sarah Leah Glass – Bernie's mum meets new family.

Clairette's training in hard work was put to use in Bernie's new engineering enterprise. She had rebelled in Baghdad after graduation and studied shorthand and typing instead of cooking and sewing. In fact, she worked and earned a living in Baghdad — something women didn't do at that time. She was Bernie's secretary but as the business grew and with the birth of their daughter Sharone, Clairette turned her attention to home. One day, on a whim, she and Bernie attended a Christie's auction in Sydney. As Clairette puts it, "I enjoyed the atmosphere and decided to attend as many auctions as possible. With an encyclopedia of Australian art in one hand and bidding with the other, I became an addict and the rest is history." She is now a member of the most formidable art dealers in Sydney. Not bad for a girl from Baghdad, never schooled in art but a very smart risk taker.

Within four years she was so enthusiastic about Sydney Harbour that she urged her parents and her sister Floty, who were still in London, to move to Australia. Australia had a "white" policy after the war and would not give immigration visas to anyone born in Iraq or countries in Asia and Africa. Since Clairette had married an Australian she had no problem. Floty decided to read Dale Carnegie's *How to Win Friends and Influence People* and with her new skills set off for the Australian Embassy in London. She told them the story of fleeing Baghdad, of going on to England, and of now being denied access to her family in Sydney. She worked on the embassy officials for six months and they eventually gave her, and her parents, Naima and David, visas to emigrate. Her sister May joined them from Israel and they set off in 1959 on the long sea voyage to another new land.

What was initially an embarking on a new life turned into a tragedy for Uncle David, who, like his grandfather Haskell, died on the ship in the Indian Ocean. In accordance with naval regulations, Naima and her children were forced to bury Uncle David at sea. It was a shattering experience for them. The captain was most sympathetic and gave Uncle David a naval burial, with his body wrapped in a Union Jack. Three other Jews on the ship prayed with the family as his body slid down into the water. Sadly, the family has no cemetery they can go to when they want to remember their father.

Naima, May, and Floty were met by Bernie and Clairette. Floty enjoyed Australia but moved to Canada, where she immediately felt at home in the Jewish community and with her future Canadian husband, Gerry Urbach, a busy doctor in Toronto. Naima traveled between Sydney, Toronto, and Boston for the remainder of her life.

The Baghdad Ezekiels in Toronto, Canada
Fred and Clairette (standing); Shoullie, Floty and May (seated, left to right)

Bernie and Clairette are now experts on the artists of Australia. They have bought and sold paintings as dealers through the years and have a fine collection in their home and the homes of their children. When they travel local museums and galleries are a must. Besides art, they consume books, movies, avant-garde theater and music, they take walks on the beach and enjoy a ritual coffee at 4p.m. every day. The grandchildren are front-and-center in their lives and they both spend many hours driving, caring for, and cooking weekly for their gang of four. They are lots of fun and we delight in one another's company. In retirement, playing and experiencing are in full tilt — when I am in their company, the enthusiasm for new information and performance is contagious.

Sisters Sophie and Mozelle with sisters May and Clairette, Sydney

May, in the meantime, has a most colorful life with her husband, Fred Stein. If you ever want to know anything about the Israel Philharmonic, ask Fred Stein. Fred intimately knows the orchestra's repertoire and many of it's musicians and conductors, past and present. Besides his love of music and his success in business, Fred's other passion is May. They met through a mutual friend who brought Fred to Floty and May's flat one day pretending that she had a book to return; Fred grabbed the book and said he would borrow it and return it the next day. Floty and May both made sure they were home as it was not clear which of them Fred liked. He was the perfect gentleman and took both sisters out for dinner that evening, confusing them even more, but very quickly it was plain that he had fallen for May. Meanwhile, their friend, Rachel Valler, is still waiting to be paid for making the match.

It was love at first sight for both. Fred had come to Sydney Harbour from Berlin. May had come to Sydney from Baghdad. With their similar interests and strong wills our family has learned that when they don't agree, Baghdad and Berlin collide. Fred has said of Clairette, Floty and May, "Bernie married the sister with the face, Gerry married the sister with the brains, and I married the body!"

Fred Stein grew up in an Orthodox home. He had a modest and happy childhood with friends from all backgrounds. He had a loving mother, Mutti, and a typically strict father, Vati, who was a traveling salesman. They had a strong allegiance to Germany. Fred's grandfather, Abraham Stein, fought in the German Army during the Franco-Prussian War as a loyal patriot and Fred's father fought for Germany in World War I. Fred attended a secular German school until 1936, when all Jewish children were expelled from public schools and he was moved to a Jewish day school for the next three years.

After 1939, German Jews were not allowed to openly practice their religion. As Fred describes it, "Vati had experienced a growing climate of hatred during his travels — in 1935 he was refused lodging at an inn when another customer refused to sleep under the same roof as a Jew. Vati saw the harsh signs ahead and wanted to leave as soon as possible where-as Mutti did not share these concerns and refused to leave Berlin, which she considered their only home." Fred has vague memories of his father's acute realization of the anti-Semitism that was growing in Germany and remembers well *Kristallnacht* on November 9, 1938, when the Nazi *brownshirts* went around to all Jewish shops and synagogues, looting them and smashing any exposed glass on the front of the buildings.

Fred's father soon discovered the true reason for his mother's unwillingness to leave Berlin. He was shocked and furious when he learned she was involved romantically with the married cantor of their synagogue. While a hue and cry went through the community, Fred recalled that his father would not give his mother a chance to explain her behavior and treated her with a cold silence until he got a divorce. Once the divorce was final, Fred, aged 12, and his father were fortunate enough to get out of Germany to England in transit to their final goal, Australia.

"I was in a turmoil of sadness to leave my mother," Fred relates, "but I felt an excitement at the idea of travel to new lands." He recalls the hatred his father expressed for his mother for years after they left Berlin and was never allowed to speak of her to his father again. "I missed her desperately. It was not the same without my beautiful mother." Instead, Fred found himself racing across Europe to escape from the Gestapo, to England, a land where the language and customs were foreign. Vati had looked farther for a place to hide from his hurt and anger, and before long they were on a ship to a new home, Sydney.

Fred learned quickly how to adapt. His youth and the new adventures helped him to move forward with optimism. Sydney proved to be the place Fred and his own family would wrap their hearts around and create happy and flourishing lives. In time, after the initial years of hard times, even Vati remarried and made a home for himself with his new wife.

Fred traveled to Germany in 1972 and 1992 to show May his old home in Berlin. They made a pilgrimage to Auschwitz, and Fred wandered the grounds for seven hours. Perhaps, he was trying to find the mother he lost. He learned of his mother's fate in 1969, when he visited New York for the first time. There he met Gunther Ruschin, an Auschwitz survivor who was the son of his mother's cantor. Gunther, by an odd chance, was visiting New York from his new home in Chile. The meeting was awkward for Fred but he wanted information about his mother. Fred feels "it was neither his fault nor mine, that his father and my mother committed adultery, which subsequently, of course, saved my life." Gunther told him that his father and Fred's mother got married in Berlin in 1940 [after Gunther's mother died of cancer] and that they lived together as a Jewish family in Berlin until the Nazis came to collect them on the 27th February, 1943, on the last transport of Jews out of Berlin to Auschwitz. It was in the middle of a bitter cold winter and the cattle train trip took several days. As soon as they arrived, Fred's mother and Gunther's sister were separated from Gunther and his father. That was the last time Gunther saw any of them. Gunther was the sole survivor.

Fred returned to Berlin in 2003 to show his sons, David and Myron, his first home. The new tenant of his former home told Fred that his mother had been deported to Auschwitz on February 27, 1943. At first very apprehensive when Fred showed up at the door, he cried quietly as he spoke. Afterwards, perhaps because of Fred's sincere and charming nature and the gift of a bottle of wine, they became good friends. When the family returned to Sydney, Fred's sons gave their father a gift — a framed piece of wire fencing they had found on the ground in Auschwitz. To this day Fred recites *Kaddish* for his mother every year.

In part because of their frequent guests, their table features bountiful tastes from all parts of the world. Two of my favorite creations are May's plum and *kugelhopf* cakes.

Lunch at Bondi Beach
Bernie Freedman – standing – a friend
Fred Stein, Clairette Freedman, May Stein, Shoullie Ezekiel – seated left to right.

‹ఠ *Hameem*

Also known in Arabic as T'BITH. It is usually served with *zalatha* and *halbah*. In Bombay, *hameem* was eaten on Saturday for lunch after we returned from the synagogue. Serves 8.

INGREDIENTS:
1 whole roasting chicken
salt and pepper to taste
1 tsp. ground turmeric
1 tsp. ground cardamom
4 medium tomatoes parboiled, peeled, and mashed
1 large carrot peeled and cut into 1" pieces and parboiled in 2 cups of water (save the water)

METHOD:
Preheat the oven to 350°F – 175°C.

Rub the chicken well with turmeric and ground cardamom; brown in a large pot over medium heat without oil. Move the chicken to a plate after browning. Add mashed tomatoes to drippings and stir quickly. Add rice to the tomatoes, stir quickly, and move rice to the side of the pot. Return chicken to the pot. Sprinkle salt, pepper on the chicken. Stir all together quickly. Gradually add carrots and water of the carrots to the pot. Add more water depending on amount of rice used (2 cups water to 1 cup rice).

Cover and cook for 1/2 hour on low to medium heat.

Once rice has absorbed all liquid place covered pot in the preheated oven for 1 hour.

Reduce oven to 250°F – 120°C and cook for 4 more hours. Chicken can cook from morning to evening at a lower heat if you will be out all day. Dinner will be ready when you return.

Some families add peeled hard-boiled eggs placed in a metal dish on top of the chicken. The eggs absorb the flavor of the chicken and come out in different shades of brown.

☜ *Chicken Bamya*

Serve with hot rice. Serves 4.

INGREDIENTS:
1 cut-up chicken
1 large yellow onion, chopped fine
2 cloves crushed garlic
salt and pepper to taste
1/2 tsp. turmeric
2 parboiled tomatoes, peeled and chopped
1/2 lbs. fresh okra (the smaller the better)
juice of 1/2 small lemon

METHOD:
Brown chicken in a pot slowly with onions and garlic and without any oil. Add salt and pepper with turmeric; continue to brown and add tomatoes; add 1/4 cup water, cover the pot, and cook on very low for a half hour.

Add 1 to 2 cups of water to the pot, cover pot, and continue cooking on very low for 1 hour. Add whole okra and lemon juice just before serving, and cook for 10-15 minutes.

(I prefer to cook the okra in whole pieces at the end to keep the vegetable al dente.)

☙ *Plum Cake*

INGREDIENTS:
3 large eggs
sugar
flour
sweet butter
2 lbs. medium red plums cored and halved

METHOD:
Place the cracked eggs in a measuring cup. Use the measurement of eggs as your measurement for sugar, butter and flour (1/2 cup of eggs would equal 1/2 cup each of sugar, butter and flour). Cut butter into pieces and place all ingredients except the plums in a large mixing bowl. Beat until smooth. Pour mixture into a well buttered 9x9" baking pan. Place plums (cut vertically) on top of cake mixture. Sprinkle with sugar.

Bake in a moderate oven (350°F or 175°C) for approx. 40-45 minutes.

ℭ Kugelhopf

INGREDIENTS:
8oz (225 gm) dark chocolate
2oz (50 gm) sweet butter
6 large eggs
2 cups (225 gm) sugar
2 cups (225 gm) self-rising flour
10 oz (275 gm) sour cream

METHOD:
Melt butter and chocolate: put both aside separately. In a large bowl, beat 6 yolks with 1 cup sugar until creamy. Add sour cream and stir; add melted butter and stir. Slowly add the flour until well blended. Beat 6 egg whites with 1 cup sugar until stiff. Add egg whites to flour mixture and combine carefully. Pour 2/3 of mixture into a well-buttered kugelhopf (or Bundt) pan. Combine the melted chocolate with remaining 1/3 flour mixture. Pour the chocolate mixture over the batter in pan. Bake at 220°F (105°C) for 10 minutes. Lower heat to 180°F (80°C) and bake for 50-55 minutes until cake feels firm and an inserted knife or skewer come out clean; cool in pan and then on a rack.

India

Part II

☙ *Beloved Bombay*

In India time has no meaning. When you make a dinner date for 7p.m., it's more common to finally eat around 9p.m. or even later. I.S.T. is the abbreviation for Indian Standard Time, but for those in the real world of India, it is known as *Indian Stretchable Time*. With the many daily diversions, how on earth could we always be on time? We were constantly distracted by the sights and sounds of India. There were the many vendors who sang out their humble occupations and whom my brother Ike and I loved to mimic. The *mochi* (shoemaker) who came around to fix our shoes and sandals would call out, "Mochi, mochi walla." He would sit on the ground on the side of our building and fix anything from torn sandals to broken heels. The paper and bottle man was known as the *battli walla*. His song was similar, "Battli, battli papar; battli, battli papar." He bought all our used paper and glass bottles. This was the earliest form of recycling in my experience. He even bought old records and the silver paper we collected in large balls from the Capstan cigarette boxes of my parents.

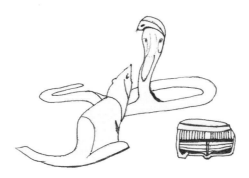

Cobra and mongoose – before the fray

Other favorite vendors were the "monkey man" and the "snake charmer," who went from house to house entertaining people. They were also to be found in the parks across the street from us, together with the "balloon man," who could magically create giraffes, ducks, monkeys, you name it, out of his balloons. The monkey man had an organ and as he played, the monkey tipped it's hat, chattering away, and then danced around the crowd with an open hat begging for money. The snake charmer usually carried a cobra in a basket that he would place on the ground. When he opened the basket and began to play his flute, the cobra would slowly unwind its way out of the basket. A less pleasant experience was when the snake charmer came with two baskets, one with a cobra and one holding a mongoose. We were told that these two creatures are natural-born enemies. Both baskets were opened up and the snake and mongoose deposited on the ground. The fight to the death was more than I could handle but I think my brothers and their friends loved it. I always thought it was a very cruel way to use animals to make a living. Before they did kill each other, they were quickly re-deposited into their basket homes.

On a much lighter note, the *Nankatti* Band, a group of well intentioned non-musicians, came to our building every month and serenaded us with more noise than music. Despite their lack of musical education, they were so sincere in their efforts that my parents always gave them money for trying.

My earliest memories of Bombay are of our ground floor flat in Colaba. My younger sister, Dinah and I were playing in the back garden one day when she decided to hide behind an old wooden cupboard propped against the outside wall of the house. She soon realized that she couldn't get out as there was no room to turn around and she started to scream. I was five and she was three and big sister, who adored her baby sister, held the cupboard away from the wall so that Dinah could get out. Mum had heard the cries and came running outside in time to see me hold the cupboard while Dinah stepped out from behind. For some unknown reason, she thought I was trying to hurt Dinah and yelled and berated me. She would not listen to my explanation, which she did not seem to believe. My sister slept constantly and sometimes I went to her crib and asked her to get up and come and play with me. She never answered and I felt lost and confused. Years later, I realized that my sister was dying of spinal meningitis; she died shortly after our garden escapade. My parents never discussed Dinah with me after that. It must have been too much for them. At the age of five, I had no idea where Dinah had gone. And felt, somehow, that I was to blame for her absence. It took me years to get over her disappearance and to understand that her death was not my fault.

We lived a comfortable life and were considered upper middle class. We moved from Colaba to a building named Firuz Ara in the Fort area which became our home from 1939 until we left India in 1952. It was well located across the street from the Oval where my brothers played cricket and football and I had classes in dressage in the early mornings on a horse named Black Beauty. My enthusiasm for riding was significantly hampered by my Viennese teacher, who loved using his crop on my boots, or so it felt to me. The grass -covered Oval was almost ten blocks long and was used by many sports teams in Bombay for football, field hockey and cricket. Giant palms ran around the entire parameter of the Oval, making it look quite grand. Field hockey was a sport I loved and I played as a right wing forward with the Bombay Grays "B" team. We were always soaked to the skin after a game and our coaches fed us sour mangoes covered with salt to quickly re-hydrate. I loved that taste.

Across the street also were the Bandstand, the Cooperage, and a football stadium where we listened to the British military band, played and went to matches of local football teams. The Cooperage was a small park with countless flower beds and flowering trees. There were benches around the outer edges of the park and under them I often found small amounts of *annas* (Indian coinage), which I spent on balloons and treats. My sister Shoshanna was always easily recognized by her cartwheel legs that were forever in the air at the Cooperage. Behind our building, within walking distance, were the Back Bay Baths where we swam almost daily. I could walk to my first school, the Convent of Jesus and Mary, with my Auntie Vicki's daughter Chun-Chun, who lived only three buildings away.

The population of Bombay at that time was over one million. The city was noisy, fast and full of life. The scent of flowers filled the air and skies were clear for miles around and we could see the

Elephanta Caves from the Gateway of Bombay. Now the population of Bombay is nearly twenty million and the skies are enveloped in smog and unhealthy particles spewed by the wood and charcoal fires that most of the poor use for cooking. It makes me sad to see these changes whenever I return to Bombay. The noisy city of my youth has become a 24/7 constancy of din. For those who are lucky enough to have air conditioning, windows are closed most of the time to keep out the pollution of decibels and dirty air.

A long hallway ran the length of our flat. During the heavy rains of the monsoons we raced back and forth in the hall, used the black and white marble squares on the floor for hopscotch, and generally drove our parents crazy. In the front were the dining room and drawing room. To the left of the hall were two bedrooms and baths that were quite spacious. The spacious bathrooms were tiled from floor to ceiling, with a shower that had no doors as water drained into holes in the floor. My parents' bath was maroon and gray, with the tub, sink and toilet in maroon ceramic. Our bath was in yellow and gray and our tub, sink and toilet were yellow ceramic—quite modern for Bombay in 1941. Our room had two four-poster beds and the two old cupboards that had been my parents' first set of furniture. The posters had mosquito nets hanging from them all year round. When Shoshanna was born she slept in my parents' room; Abe, Ike and I slept in the other bedroom, on the beds pushed together. We were all under ten years then and had constant pillow fights and a lot of jumping competitions on those two beds. Not very conducive to sleep but, luckily for our *ayahs* (nannies), we finally slept, happily exhausted with the multitude of activities of every wonderful day.

On the right side of the hallway was the "milk" kitchen, where breakfast, tea and desserts were prepared. Here water was boiled daily and strained into a large red clay urn on a stand called a *mutka*. Due to water shortages, we could use the tap water only during certain hours of the day and purifying water had to be properly planned. A small stove, large baskets of fruit, and a *cuppayra* (a cupboard with netted doors that kept cakes and the white cheese stored in bottles cool and fresh) were all housed in this kitchen. We never ate in the kitchen. Usually we ate on the run during the day, in our bedroom, or with our parents in the dining room.

Our flat was on the ground floor, with our front door on the left side of the lift in the foyer of the building. The black and white marble floors were cleaned and disinfected daily by the *meythur*, to keep ahead of the never-ending armies of ants, cockroaches and lizards. We had to shake our shoes out every morning before putting them on in case a lizard or cockroach had embedded itself in the hospitality of our shoes. And during the monsoons we put newspaper in our shoes to keep *papandi* (mildew) from forming. The *meythur* was of the "untouchable" class as were all workers who cleaned bathrooms and floors. Fortunately, things changed after India's independence in 1947 and, with the emergence of new ideas and laws regarding class restrictions, his son was attending college in Bombay by 1952.

We had many servants. Compared with our life in America, we were highly indulged. But in India almost everyone had servants. There were many poor and uneducated villagers who came to the cities to make money and send their earnings to their families back home to pay for their farm property. Many servants returned to their *mooluck* (hometown) when they were old. It was a system that has been part of this society for generations. And, of course, our servants were very much a part of our family. We were always taught to listen to them and they were in charge when our parents were not home.

At the end of the hall on the right was a small room where our servants stored their personal items and took baths. This was their only private space. Our three women servants, Lucy, Esthoo, and Alice, slept on the floor nearest the child each was responsible for. Outside the back door a small hall led to the main kitchen, where lunches and dinners were prepared by our cook, Vincent. My mother taught him to make all our favorite Iraqi dishes and he became an expert. He had a helper who came every day to grind up the spices into a *masala* on a heavy flat stone with a small stone rolling pin. Masala is a mixture of spices used as the base for most curries. Vincent was tall for an Indian male, about 5'10", and slim and handsome. He knew he was handsome and was a flirt around the women servants. His flirtations with our *ayah* Esthoo led to a marriage, and they left our employ to return to their original home in Goa. Vincent was a great loss to us, and since we were heading out of the country soon my mother didn't hire another cook. After Vincent left I began to learn about cooking by watching my mother, a superb cook. She was shocked at my initiation, when tears poured down my face as I sliced onions. Much to her consternation, I became an expert at cutting onions on the bias, both thick and thin.

The men servants slept away from the flat, including Mohammed, our driver. He was gray-haired, with a large curled moustache, and his western style jacket over baggy white cotton pants was as close to a uniform as any of the servants wore. He took meticulous care of our car and watched over us as if we were his grandchildren. He often saved us from the downpour of the monsoon rains with a large black umbrella.

Each day began with school. Abe and I went to the Convent (boys were there only for kindergarten which was based on the Montessori method). I continued at the Convent while Abe and Ike attended the Cathedral Boys School, a Church of England school, until we left for England in 1946. Many missionaries in India set up private schools for the middle class but we were never under any pressure to adopt their religions. The missionary schools in the big cities were expensive, and as they relied on the Catholic, Hindu, Jewish, Muslim and Parsi populations for their students, they were very careful never to mention religion, although we saw the Catholic girls go to church during the day or on special feast days.

The cook and Mum planned the following day's menu after dinner. He would do all the accounting for the daily expenses and would then get more money for the next day's food. He and the other servants were paid monthly. Most of them could not read or write and signed their names with a thumbprint after receiving their cash for the month. Even the gardener in the Cooperage across the street got paid for bringing us fresh flowers twice a week. By the age of ten I was arranging the flowers in vases; there have been fresh flowers throughout my home ever since.

Two vital workers who came and went were the *dhobi* (laundry man) and the *darzee* (tailor). The *dhobi* came weekly, taking all our laundry and returning it folded in large sacks. I learned to count each sock, pant and shirt, mark the numbers down, and then made a recount when the clothing returned sparkling clean the next week. The *dhobi* carried many loads of dirty clothes to the countryside, where he washed them in a river and beat them clean on rocks. There were many smashed buttons to be re-sewn by yours truly. Lucy hand-washed and ironed my mother's fine lingerie and our special frocks, which looked as if they had come back from the finest French laundry.

The *darzee* usually came twice a year, before the school term and six months later. He would sit on the floor for days at a time with his hand-driven sewing machine and sew all our school uniforms and everyday play clothes. My mother would give him material and photos she cut out of American magazines of designs she wanted and, voila, it was done. He made the prettiest cotton dresses for me, often out of fabrics that we bought from a Chinese merchant who pedaled his bicycle around town. Whenever he showed up my mum and I would go into the drawing room with him. He would sit on the floor and roll out his fabric, which included Stoffels voiles, Egyptian cottons, and Swiss appliqued lace cottons that my mother loved to buy for my sister and me. This was our personal trunk show.

Lucy, our most loyal and trustworthy *ayah*, lived with us the entire time Firuz Ara was our home. A plain looking woman and meticulously clean, she wound her long hair in a tight bun and wore a crisp white sari with a simple border. She had an uncanny intuition about my friends and would mutter under her breath when someone came over whom she did not trust. I was often quite angry at her but eventually learned that she was usually right. She often controlled us with fear of the "bogeyman" and it took me years to not be afraid in the dark.

Lucy worked every day, with only Sunday mornings off for church. She earned about Rs.150 a month (approximately $15 at that time) and was fed and clothed by my mother. For Christmas and special occasions, such as the birthday of one of my siblings, she received a gold bangle. There was no gift better than gold jewelry in India and, of course, it had to be *sathanu* (98% pure gold). The lure of *soona* (gold) has endured through the last 2,000 years. People in Asia and the Middle East often trust gold more than banks. Women, in particular, were given gold, as few of them could own land. Their gold was their personal wealth and they could wear it and move with it. Lucy was so well trusted that she knew the combination of my mother's safe, which was kept on top of the dirty clothes hamper in the children's bathroom. I recall Lucy and my mum filling the safe with small gold bars that had been left with us for safe-keeping by one of my parents' friends.

Gold has consistently been a prime liquid asset throughout Asia. If you needed cash, you took gold to a gold merchant and within an hour you would receive cash for your *sathanu* based on its weight and the most up-to-date price on the London or New York exchanges. Little or no value was given to the design or craft of jewelry. Only the weight of the gold counted. In the mid to late 1940s many Jews, fleeing Afghanistan, arrived penniless but with plenty of gold jewelry under the layers of their women's clothes. European refugees during World War II also kept gold on their persons, and some were lucky to have diamonds to bargain for their survival.

Mohammed took Lucy and me on a drive once to a large round dirt enclosure walled on all sides. This arena held criminals waiting for sentencing. Lucy's son was there for robbery and she was delivering a package of money to his guards to protect her son from other men in the compound. She was furious with her son and I was shocked at the crude prison facility, with a variety of villains from all walks of life housed in a large open space together. What a contrast to the Midnight Mass she and I went to in a similar compound, but one without walls. She took me to the Oval one Christmas Eve where thousands of Catholics, each holding a lit candle, were praying and singing. It was my first experience of Christmas and I feel it was the purest manifestation of what the celebration was about. On my first journey back to Bombay in 1969 I searched for Lucy but sadly did not find her anywhere.

My friend Zareen lived next door and we both attended the Convent School. She was one of the older students and yet we became good friends. Besides sharing comic books and piano lessons with Mother Martha, our greatest fun was throwing water balloons from the terrace of Zareen's building on the British soldiers on the street below. They never knew where the flying balloons came from. This was during World War II and the fight for Indian independence. I remember seeing British privates refuse to salute Indian colonels.

One day I was invited by one of my English friends to go to the Breach Candy Swim Club. This was on Malabar Hill in the posh section of Bombay and I was excited to get a chance to swim there. Only whites were allowed and the front gate was guarded by an Indian man. When we got there the guard told me I could not go in. I guessed I was not white enough. What a shock and embarrassment for me. That was my first and last time at this fancy club. Discrimination was evident everywhere and there was a clear awareness of the unfair ways of the British. We were all for Indian independence from the United Kingdom and had a high regard for Lord Mountbatten, who put together the final papers of sovereignty for the Indian people.

Parents and children in drawing room

Shortly after we moved to Firuz Ara, my mother had a dream. Someone gave her a glass of lime juice and said, "Drink this." The next day she told Dad and his brother, Sonny, about the dream and asked to see the racing sheet. There was a horse named Lime Juice with 10 to 1 odds. Both Dad and Uncle Sonny pooh-poohed her decision to bet on Lime Juice. She told me, "I bet everything I had on the tote and with the bookies and ended up winning at 8 to 1 odds. She won 30,000 rupees and furnished our entire flat with custom-made Burmese teak furniture, every piece finished with rounded edges to keep us safe when we raced around the house.

Uncle Sonny loved the horses

Every Saturday during the season, my parents went to the Mahalakshmi race course. They knew many of the owners and jockeys and were often given the inside word when the races were rigged. They both loved to gamble but Mum was lucky and Dad seldom won. Dad and Uncle Sonny never quite got over her luck and neither did they trust her intuition over their systems. Never that I know of did they win anything like Mum. Mum recalls that when the race was over and she was clapping her hands exuberantly, Dad turned to her and said, "For God's sake don't do that. It hurts." We heard about Lime Juice for years. One of my many childhood confusions was when Dad came home and said, "He broke the record." My imagination portrayed an elegant Arabian horse stomping on a 78, as one stomped a glass at a wedding.

Our big treat was going to the races with them on Gymkhana Day, when children were welcomed. Everyone dressed to the nines for the races and it was fun to see all manner of costumes and finery. Dad wore a white sharkskin suit while Mum usually had a stylish outfit made at Auntie Rae's dress shop, with hat and jewelry to match. They were such a good-looking couple that it made me proud. High society was evident everywhere, with maharajahs and maharanis the primary horse owners. The vibrant colors of the saris were only overshadowed by the large vivid rubies, sapphires, and emeralds that glistened around the bookie's ring. I was given money to bet with and sometimes taken down to the "ring" to see the horses make the rounds before a race. Often, one uncle or the other would give me a tip to bet on a horse, but I don't remember ever winning much.

Some people had their own boxes and sometimes we were invited to the box used by Howard Donovan, the American consul, and his wife, Margaret. They were very good friends of my parents and loved to come to our home for Arabic food and music. One Gymkhana Day when Mum was pregnant with my sister Shoshanna, we were sitting with the Donovans in their box. My mother was very angry with Mahatma Gandhi for stating in the morning Times of India that the Jewish victims of the Holocaust should accept their karma. She was a great admirer of Gandhi's and could not understand his insensitivity. She said she would never accept the killing of her family.

As she spoke with the Donovans, a short, very tanned American man entered their box. He was struck by my mother's beauty and asked her where she had been all his life. My mother responded, "Avoiding creeps like you." The American was visibly embarrassed and excused himself to place a bet. Donovan turned to my mother and told her that she had just insulted Vinegar Joe Stilwell the head of all U.S. forces in the Burma/India arenas. Upset, Mum quickly apologized to him when he came back, and then, she too went off to make a bet. She found out later that he was so struck by her directness, he instructed Donovan to put aside six numbers for U.S. immigration in our names. At that time only 100 people could emigrate to America from India each year and it probably helped us that my father was a British subject born in Burma. I recall going to the American Consulate in London in 1947, when I was too young to understand how unusual it was that six immigration numbers were waiting for us. Many years later I realized what a valuable gift we had received from Vinegar Joe.

❧ *Crawford Market*

I loved going to Bombay's open-air Crawford Market as a little girl. This affinity lasted throughout my childhood in Bombay and I returned to Crawford Market every time I traveled back to India from America as an adult. The market spanned ten square blocks and was the source of most of our food. Chickens, lamb and fresh vegetables were purchased there by our cook, Vincent, every day, and my Mother and I went weekly to buy a variety of fruit, staples and specialty products. Everyone shopped at Crawford Market: the urban housewife with servant in tow, the young teacher rushing through a busy day, men in *dhotis*, women in saris and Punjabi dress, the various Europeans in the class of the Raj. They mingled under the same open roofs amid a cacophony of sound and total bedlam. No one strolled at Crawford Market. We raced through to avoid the constant yelling and cajoling of the shop-keepers. Radios with energetic Indian music blared from the stalls along the aisles.

Brightly colored canopies with signs in both English and Hindi advertising the merchandise of the shopkeepers. They were usually painted on cloth in bright oranges, reds, greens and black. Various *patheelas* (pots) made out of thin stainless steel, in every size imaginable, from large rice pots with covers to the small brass *dal-las* for Turkish coffee, hung from the ceilings. The interior walls were covered with tins and boxes of imported foods. The merchants stood out front or sat on cushions facing the walkway and would dive into their closet-size stalls and bring out the items we wanted. We shopped for hard-to-find specialties from Britain, Europe, China, and America that included, Heinz ketchup, cheeses, canned sockeye salmon (my dad's favorite), Kellogg's Corn Flakes and Nabisco Shredded Wheat (another of his favorites). During the 1940s there were very few choices from foreign markets because India had very little hard currency (dollars) to use for luxury items.

Our driver, Mohammed, took us to the market. Driving from our flat in the Back Bay area of Bombay to the market we were engulfed by the constant honking of car horns, by cows ambling through the streets, and by pedestrians walking alongside the cars and bicycle rickshaws, rather than on the sidewalk. I realize now that the trucks with their mysterious "Please Honk" signs were warning these pedestrians to get out of the way. The drive got us in the mood for the hectic nature of our day's marketing.

Photo by Craig Dequadros, Ace Productions Pvt. Ltd.

There's my basket wallah

The first thing we did was to hire for a pittance, one of the many boys and men whose job it was to carry our purchases in large baskets on their heads. Typically barefoot or in sandals, this person who might be anything from a young boy to a gray haired senior, would follow us around the market as we filled his basket. When it was full, he would disappear. No matter where we were in this huge bazaar, he would find us with an empty basket on top of his head to carry more packages. When we returned to our car, all our purchases were in the trunk.

Photo by Craig Dequadros, Ace Productions Pvt. Ltd.

Fruit vendors – look for the grenade-like custard apple

Exploring the fruit area of the market was an adventure I often shared with my father, who taught me how to pick out the best. We went up and down each of the many rows of oranges, small and large mangoes (we bought only Alfonso mangoes, which were considered "the king of fruit"), red, yellow, and green bananas and custard apples, whose dirty knobby dark green surface resembles a grenade. Behind each knob lies a long, thin black seed coated with a layer of white custard, delicate to the palate and satisfying after a heavy meal. There were chickoos, small round brown fruits that look like kiwi and have a meaty interior as sweet as any baked dessert. Apples came from the northern parts of India, as did gooseberries, which my paternal granny, Hannah, used for her delicious gooseberry jam.

Dad would walk up and down the aisles bargaining, while the fruit vendors shouted, "Sa'ab, Sa'ab, try my mango." The market fruit stands resembled rainbows in bold color, with tastes to match. Dad had his usual vendors but always kept them honest by checking others. This was considered the way to buy, and both seller and buyer would have been adrift without this informal protocol. Since we drank fresh orange juice every morning, we needed lots of oranges. We usually purchased these, and all other fruit, by the basket, each of which held three to five dozen.

Bustling Crawford Market – Bombay

One drawback of Crawford Market's abundance was that we ate too many mangoes and got ugly "mango boils" on our faces. The local cure for these was to wash your face with fresh rain-water which our servants collected in buckets outside our flat. Guavas, breadfruit, papayas and other fruits too numerous to mention were in season most of the year, so our fruit intake was nothing less than fabulous. Is it any wonder that fresh fruit was the main dessert in India?

When I was about 14, my mother would hand me 100 rupees, close to $100 in today's purchasing power, and send me off to Crawford Market with a list. I had to keep within a budget. Perhaps she was passing on to me the advice she had received from Mahatma Gandhi, for whom she worked while he was jailed by the British in Poona. When she told Gandhi that she was going to marry, he said, "My child, do not spend more than your husband's income."

Within months of my fifteenth birthday, I was tasked with planning the next day's dinner with the cook. It was part of what was expected of me – to get married, have a home, have children and be an *eschet chayil* (virtuous woman). I often resented the "training" but now I'm grateful for it. This informal education certainly gave me the skills I needed to deal with my life as a homemaker. My brothers were never taught any of this. The men were expected to earn the money so the women could buy the food; the buying was women's work. Most of the men were traders when I lived in India, but gradually the younger generations were educated in other professions. And not just the men, but the women too. What has never changed is that the men are expected to protect their wives and children and to protect the good name of the family.

Dad never cooked, but he learned to bake when he worked in the oilfields of Burma after his family lost their money. Every now and then he would bake the best pound cake I've ever eaten (still my mother's favorite cake). My favorite was *kahi*, a sweet, fried, highly caloric pancake made during the feast of Shavuoth, the commemoration of the Jewish people receiving the Torah.

We did not get all of our food from the Crawford Market. Every morning the milkman and the egg man brought fresh milk and eggs to the back door. We tested the eggs in a bucket of water: if they floated, they were bad; if they sank to the bottom of the pail, they were okay to eat. The milk arrived in huge tin pails by train from the countryside. Our bearer boiled the fresh milk every day and saved the *malai* (cream). When we kids came home from school we clamored for the cream, which we spread on fresh crusts that were then sprinkled with cocoa. This was our idea of heaven. Fresh crusty bread, a lot like typical French bread, was delivered to the front door every morning.

With our afternoon tea there were always *machboos*, *ka-a-kas* and *babas*. And lots of *jibbin* (fresh feta cheese), which was plaited or in blocks and stored in large bottles of water and salt in the milk kitchen. These were all made by an Iraqi Jewish woman named Sameha. She looked like a little gnome with a terribly bent-over body. Sameha supported her daughter and grandchild and worked constantly. I visited her tiny flat once and found it dismal and poor with no space to sit down. The entire place was organized for work. There was nothing that would provide comfort.

Sameha had weekly orders with many of the Jewish Baghdadi households. For Rosh Hashanah and Yom Kippur she was especially busy. She wrapped the orders in large pieces of cloth and delivered her packages walking from house to house in the hot sun. Vincent made meat and vegetable *samosas* at home and Sameha made all the cheese *samosas*, or *sambusak* as it is known in Arabic. She was the only source for our favorite Iraqi pastries and plaited feta cheese, in all of Bombay.

Sameha was also the *dalal* (matchmaker) in our community. When I turned 16 she came with offers of marriage and I deliberately disappeared. To me it was a humiliation to even imagine an arranged marriage. Usually a dowry was involved and Sameha would get a small commission. Unfortunately for her, she never made money from my family this way.

In Bombay, during the war, we had a few Jewish European bakers who had fled to India. We bought their cakes for special occasions like birthdays and weddings. One of them, Mr. Sprung, made chocolates that were the best I have ever eaten. He walked door to door around Bombay, red faced and perspiring, with a briefcase full of Sprung chocolates. He quickly became famous as a *chocolatier* and was one of the many success stories of saved Jews.

We were constantly receiving trays of sweets and flowers from different friends - Hindus, Muslims, Parsis - on their religious holidays. These wonderful treats included fireworks, and because just about everyone celebrated all the various religious holidays, we had many days off from school and lots of fireworks. Our universe consisted of friends from every religion and from many countries and none of us felt that one was better than the other.

Our cuisine was as multicultural as our friends. Dishes ranged from *shoofta* (ground meat kebabs), *marag* (Baghdadi chicken soup), fried pomfret, very hot and spicy curries, potato chops, *kitchri* (hot rice mixed with cooked lentils and served with yogurt), *hamad* (beets cooked like a soup with chicken or lamb), roast chicken and potatoes and last but not least, Southern fried chicken, which we added to our menu after living in America for a year in 1947. The desserts included floating island pudding, *blancmange* pudding, chocolate pudding and jello or fruit during very hot weather.

Dinner guests on Friday nights included Jewish Syrian bachelors who were traders in Bombay during the war. There were usually 10 to 12 of us at the table. *Kadoos* (wine) was made from fresh grapes that had been parboiled, then hand-squeezed through a fine cloth by me (since I was the eldest daughter). There was always roast chicken and *aloomakala*, beetroot or *bamya kooba* and *arook* (stuffed rice balls) for special guests. After we had eaten fish or spicy finger foods, we washed our hands in warm lemon water set in small bowls at each of our places. Dessert on Sabbath was usually fresh fruit. This was my dad's favorite and he personally peeled, cut, and passed around fruit to everyone at the table. This is one of my fondest memories of my father. I miss his sweet smile as he looked at each one of us and asked, "Would you like a slice of apple?" I miss this tender exchange as I miss our kissing and wishing one another "Shabbat Shalom."

Cooking our family recipes takes me back to the din of the Crawford Market and to my happy life in Bombay. I am nostalgic for that time when I was young and life uncomplicated. During my travels in other countries since then I have visited many markets, and I always compare them with the Crawford Market. Nothing feels the same or looks the same, nor do any of the other places evoke the comfort and the longing to walk and shop along the colorful and boisterous aisles of our Bombay market. The man who carried my many purchases on his head beats a shopping cart any day. Anyone who enters the rich territory of masses of fruit and vegetables, dry goods and crowing live chickens is bombarded with a chorus of life. I love Crawford Market best.

On my visit in 1969, I especially remember young men who carried large boom boxes under their arms and played them full blast, adding to the cacophony of the market. Other men would look at them with a smirk and giggle. Navin Patel, my cousin Lulu's husband, explained to me that the Indian government encouraged the practice of birth control by men, and those who had vasectomies were given a boom box as a reward. I was amused that the onlookers seemed to be saying, "We know what you did."

෪ *Kahi*

Similar in consistency to parathas, layered fried bread.
Serve with tea or coffee. 20 servings.

INGREDIENTS:
2 lbs. unbleached flour 900gm.
2 tsp. salt
1 lb. melted butter 450gm.
1 to 1-1/2 cups water

METHOD:
Combine flour and salt in a bowl. Add 4 tablespoons butter, rubbing in with fingertips until mixture resembles fine bread crumbs. Add 1 cup water and knead until it forms into a soft dough. If too dry, add a little more water and knead until the dough comes away from the sides of the bowl. Knead until dough is smooth and elastic. Cover and set aside for one hour.

Divide dough into 20 pieces. Shape into balls the size of a small orange.

Roll each ball into a thin disk shape. Brush each round with a little of the remaining butter. Fold the rounds in half and then into quarters. Roll again into rounds. Repeat process of brushing butter and folding 3 or 4 times. Shape into balls again. Cover with a damp tea towel until ready to fry. Pat or flatten into rounds and fry in butter until golden brown in a nonstick pan. Add a little butter to the pan each time.

 *Pearl's Marag*

Baghdadi Jewish chicken soup. A cure-all. 3-4 servings.

INGREDIENTS:
1 small chicken, cut up and skinned
1 tsp. turmeric
1/2 tsp. each garlic powder and ginger powder
salt and pepper to taste
2 medium skinned tomatoes parboiled, peeled and mashed
2 plus cups water
6 peeled and cut-up carrots

METHOD:
In a large pot, brown chicken quickly on medium heat for 15-20 min; add all spices to chicken; add mashed tomatoes and keep stirring; cook on low for 20 min. Add water to cover chicken plus 2 more cups. Cook, covered, on low to medium for 40 min. Add carrots or any other preferred vegetables. Continue to cook for another 30 min. Serve with boiled basmati rice.

ℭℨ *Shoofta*

It is customary to eat with pita and *zalatha* (tomato salad). 6-8 servings.

INGREDIENTS:
1 lb. (450 gm) ground lean sirloin
1 lb. (450 gm) ground lean lamb
4 to 5 scallions finely chopped
1 cup chopped parsley or cilantro
Juice of 1/2 lemon
1 tsp. crushed garlic
1/2 tsp. turmeric
salt & pepper to taste

METHOD:
Mix all ingredients and divide into 16 portions. Shape each portion in the shape of a cigar on a skewer, and broil over charcoal or in the oven for a total of 7-10 min. Turn on both sides. Serve with hot rice or warm pita.

ℭℨ *Zalatha*

Dice 6-8 medium tomatoes; add juice of 1/2 lemon and freshly chopped parsley or cilantro. Enjoy as a garnish on *shoofta* and pita bread.

 # *Kitchri*

A healthy, easy meal in hot weather. 6-8 servings.

INGREDIENTS:
2 cups (454 gm) red lentils
2 cups rice
1 large finely chopped yellow onion
2 crushed garlic cloves
1/2 tsp. turmeric
1 tsp. cumin
1/4 cup fresh chopped coriander

METHOD:
Wash lentils in hot water, constantly removing the white foam that develops. Cook the lentils slowly in 4 cups of water until they resemble a mush. Cook two cups of rice.

In a large frying pan, brown the onion, adding garlic and spices. Add the cooked lentils; mix well with the rice and cook covered on low for 1/2 hour. Serve with yogurt.

☙ *Mahasha*

Great with a tossed green salad. Can be frozen and reheated. 6 servings.

INGREDIENTS:
2 large torpedo onions (or 4 smaller ones)
1 1/2 cups (340 gm) cooked rice
1 lb. (454 gm) ground beef
1 lb. (454 gm) ground lamb
1/3 cup (80 ml) chopped parsley
2 tsp. (10 ml) salt
1/4 tsp. (1 ml) ground pepper
4 Tbsp. brown sugar
juice of 1/2 lemon
1/2 large tomato, coarsely chopped
2 to 4 cloves garlic, smashed
1/4 cup (60 ml) olive oil
2 large tomatoes, parboiled, peeled and chopped

METHOD:
Put the onions in a saucepan (no need to peel), cover them with water and bring them to boil. Boil the onions gently for 1 hour, adding more water as necessary to keep them covered. Drain the onions and cover them with cold water. Let them cool in the water for 30 minutes, or until they are cool enough to handle.

To make the stuffing, combine the remaining ingredients, except the olive oil and 2 large tomatoes. Mix well.

Cut off the stem end of the onions. Slit one side of each onion lengthwise from top to bottom. Do not cut all the way through so as to leave a full pocket to stuff. Gently separate onion layers and put aside on paper towels to dry. Use the larger layers to enclose the stuffing. Reserve the core of the onions for later.

Preheat oven to 325°F (165°C).

Hold an onion layer in the palm of your hand and fill it with stuffing so that you can close the onion with the edges overlapping, then set aside until all layers are stuffed.

Chop the onion cores and brown in olive oil in a large, ovenproof, flat, deep pan. Add the chopped large tomatoes and saute for 30 minutes. Remove from heat and lay the stuffed onion layers over the onion-tomato mixture, then sprinkle a little bit of the mixture over the top and also sprinkle 3/4 cup (180 ml) of water. Cover with foil and bake for 1 1/2 - 2 hours.

Other vegetables such as squash, cucumbers and tomatoes can be cooked like the onions. Only the outer skin of the vegetable is stuffed and cooked.

☙ *Potato Chops*

These can be served with a freshly tossed green salad. This is a labor-intensive recipe, but the potato chops freeze well and can be prepared in advance and cooked just prior to a meal. 6-8 servings.

INGREDIENTS:
8 large peeled potatoes
8 scallions, chopped very fine.
1 lb. (450 gm) each ground lamb & sirloin beef (or ground breast of chicken)
3 large cloves garlic, smashed
1 tsp. ground ginger
1 Tbsp. each chopped cilantro and parsley
1/2 tsp. each cumin and turmeric
2 lightly beaten eggs
1 cup (227 gm) bread crumbs

METHOD:
First boil peeled potatoes, mash them well with salt to taste. Leave in refrigerator to cool.

In a frying pan with olive oil, fry the chopped scallions for 2-3 minutes. Add the chopped meat and spices, making sure the meat has no lumps. Cook on low to medium heat quickly and stir in chopped parsley. Pour cooked meat into a large colander to allow accumulated liquid to drain out. Put meat aside to cool. While meat is cooling, shape mashed potato into 12 15 balls (tennis ball size). Place each ball in the palm of your hand, and hollow out to make room for meat filling.

Place approximately a heaping tablespoon of meat into the hollow of the potato ball and close so no meat is showing. Dip potato balls into beaten eggs and then roll onto the bread crumbs. Leave in the refrigerator on a flat plate for 15 minutes. Fry on low to medium heat in olive oil gently moving the potato chops so that they don't stick to the frying pan.

The potato chops can be baked instead of fried at 350°F (165°C). for 30 minutes.

♋ *Curries*

I use different onions and spices depending on the kind of curry I'm cooking. Choose the chilies for your taste, based on how hot you want your curry.

♋ *Chicken Curry*

Feeds 2-4 depending on appetites. Can be prepared in advance.

INGREDIENTS:
1 large finely chopped yellow onion
2-3 smashed and peeled garlic cloves
1 medium tomato, peeled, boiled and mashed
2-4 chopped chilies (depending on taste)
salt and pepper
1/2 tsp. each turmeric, cumin and coriander
1 small (2-3 lbs.) cut-up chicken
You can add 8-12 small peeled potatoes

METHOD:
Brown the onions in oil; gradually add chilies, garlic and other spices; add tomato; then add chicken, and mix thoroughly on low to medium heat; once mixed, turn heat to low and cover; chicken will cook in its own juices; check and slowly add about 1/2 cup of water; cook for 1 hour on low heat. Serve with boiled rice.

 *Fish Curry*

4 servings.

INGREDIENTS:
2 lbs. (1 kg) cut up (1-2" cubes) halibut, barramunda, red snapper, or other fleshy fish.

Use all the same ingredients as the Chicken Curry but you can choose to leave out the tomatoes and add 1/2 cup of canned coconut milk in the final cooking.

METHOD:
Follow instructions for chicken curry sauce, add the fish and cook on low to medium heat for 30 minutes. I sometimes spread my cousin Becky's Lemon Pickle (pg. 188) on the fish and cook covered for 30 minutes on low.

‿ *Beef Curry – Vindaloo*

A cold, crisp romaine salad complements the spicy vindaloo. 6 servings

---

INGREDIENTS:
2 lbs. (1 kg) stew beef cut into 1-2" cubes
1/2 tsp. ground cumin
1/2 tsp. ground coriander
1/2 tsp. (2 ml) cinnamon sticks
1 Tbsp. ground ginger
1 Tbsp. ground garlic
4-6 fresh cut-up chilies
salt & pepper to taste
1 Tbsp. red vinegar
2 large finely chopped red onions
Olive oil

I add 8-12 pieces of dried apricots to complement the strong vindaloo spices.

METHOD:
Marinate the meat with all spices and vinegar for 1 hour.

Brown onions slowly in olive oil until golden brown, then add the meat. When the meat is browned on all sides, add the chilies. Cook on a low flame for 3-4 hours and stir often to avoid burning. Add cut-up dried apricots, if desired, in last hour of cooking

Serve with hot cooked white rice.

ℭℨ *Machboos*

This is the basic recipe for *machboos* (dough). It is used by our family to make the recipes that follow, which are of both Arab and Indian origin. Most kosher homes substitute oil or margarine when making the chicken *samosas*. This recipe takes a full day but is definitely worth it.

INGREDIENTS:
2 Tbsp. active dry yeast
2 cups warm water
2 lbs. (908 gm) unbleached flour
1/2 lb. (227 gm) butter or margarine
3/4 tsp. salt
1 Tbsp. Ground anise

METHOD:
Mix yeast in a little over one cup of warm water. Cover and put aside for half an hour.

Place flour in a large mixing bowl. Work margarine or butter, salt and anise into the flour by hand or using a food processor. Add risen yeast slowly to the flour, mixing thoroughly. Knead dough together into a ball, adding water as needed, on a lightly floured surface. Put dough back into the mixing bowl and cover with heavy towels. Let dough rise for an hour and knead again; then cover and let it rise for another hour.

KA-A-KA:
Round rings of dough that are eaten with tea —add 1 Tbsp. caraway seeds to the **machboos** in the initial mixing.

Roll rings of dough onto lightly floured baking pan. Bake for 15-20 min at 325°F (165°C).

BABAS:
Round patties filled with dates that have been cooked in water and then mashed. Add 1 tsp. ground anise to the *machboos* in the initial mixing.

Make small (golf) balls of dough and roll into round circles. Create a flat round pastry: place 1 Tbsp. mashed dates on one round circle; cover with another circle of dough and pinch all around at the edges; pat one side of pastry onto a bed of sesame seeds.

Bake for 12-15 min on each side in a 325°F (165°C). oven.

‪ca‬ *Chicken Samosas*

The uncooked samosas can be frozen to cook another time. Makes a
great fast picnic or dinner with salad. 8 servings.

INGREDIENTS:
1 recipe machboos (substitute margarine for butter in a kosher home)
3 scallions, chopped fine
4 chicken breasts, chopped into 1/2" cubes
1/4 tsp. dill, chopped fine
1/2 Tbsp. crushed garlic
1/4 cup parsley, chopped fine
dash lemon juice
salt and pepper

METHOD:
Brown scallions in olive oil to golden. Add chicken and brown for 10 minutes.
Add garlic and all spices and brown for 5 minutes. Sprinkle with lemon juice.
Cool in refrigerator for 1 hour.

Roll out the dough in circles, stuff each circle with chicken mixture and shape
into half moon patties. These can be fried to golden brown in olive oil (not
too hot) or baked for 40 minutes at 325°F (165°C).

∂ Vegetable Samosas

Again, the uncooked *samosas* can be frozen to cook another time.
Different veggies can be used in season. 8 servings.

INGREDIENTS:
1 recipe *machboos*
6 large potatoes, peeled and chopped into 1" squares
1 cauliflower, cut into 1" pieces
1 cup fresh green peas
4-6 carrots, peeled and chopped into 1/2 inch pieces
12 scallions, chopped
2 Tbsp. garlic, smashed
1/4 tsp. each cumin and coriander
1/2 tsp. turmeric
4 small green chilies, chopped fine
salt and pepper

METHOD:
Parboil the potatoes, cauliflower and carrots for 5 minutes.
Brown scallions in olive oil to golden. Add chilies and brown. Add garlic and
all spices and brown 5 min. Add vegetables one at a time with the peas last
and brown 10 minutes. Put all the cooked vegetables into a colander to
drain liquid for 1/2 hour over sink. Cool in refrigerator for over 1 hour.

Roll out the dough in circles, stuff each circle with vegetable mix, and shape
into half-moon patties. These can be fried to golden brown in olive oil (not
too hot) or baked for 40 min at 325°F (165°C).

ೞ *Cheese Sambusak*

Half-moon patties filled with feta cheese and eggs that are eaten with tea – add caraway seeds to *machboos* in the initial mixing. If for a main meal, make them much larger and serve with a green salad. Smaller-sized cheese *sambusaks* are great hors d'oeuvres for a party.

INGREDIENTS:
1 recipe **machboos** made with 1/4 cup of caraway seeds
1 lb. (450 gm) feta, mashed
1-2 eggs, beaten

METHOD:
Make golf ball-sized balls of dough. Flatten balls into small round circles. Mix 1/4 of the beaten eggs at a time with feta mixture so that it is solid and not runny. Stuff each piece of dough with 1-1/2 Tbsp. cheese and egg combination. Shape into half-moons and pinch closed. Brush Sambusaks lightly with any leftover egg before baking. Bake for 12-15 min on each side at 325°F (165°C).

❀ *Hamad*

This is Iraqi borscht. Great for a cold day. 6 servings.

INGREDIENTS:
2 large, finely chopped red onions
2-3 large garlic cloves, peeled and mashed
2 Tbsp. olive oil
2-1/2 lbs. (approx. 1 kg) boneless lamb cut into 1-1/2" (1-1/2 cm) cubes
3/4 tsp. turmeric
salt and pepper to taste
1 large tomato, parboiled, peeled and mashed
4 medium beets peeled and cut into 1-1/2" (1-1/2 cm) cubes
Juice of 1/2 lemon

METHOD:
Lightly brown the onions and garlic in oil. Add meat and brown while sprinkling with all the spices. Gradually add mashed tomato stirring constantly. Cover the pot and let simmer for 1 hour, occasionally sprinkling with water to avoid burning.

Cook for 1-1/2 to 2 hours on low until lamb is tender. Add the beets and enough water to cover the meat and beets Add the lemon juice. Cook on low-medium for 1/2 hour. Serve with boiled rice.

❧ *Floating Island Pudding*

6-8 servings.

INGREDIENTS:
5 eggs
1/2 cup plus 6 Tbsp. sugar
1/4 tsp. salt
1 qt. (940 ml) scalded milk
1 tsp. vanilla

METHOD:
Slightly beat together 3 egg yolks and 2 whole eggs. Add 1/2 cup of sugar and the salt, mix well, and add hot milk gradually, stirring constantly. Cook mixture in top of double boiler until it coats the spoon, stirring constantly. Add 1/4 tsp. vanilla. Pour into a 3" deep casserole dish or individual ramekins.

Beat 3 egg whites until foamy. Beat in additional 6 Tbsp. sugar gradually. Add 3/4 tsp of vanilla. Using a large spoon, drop meringue onto hot custard, tightly cover pan until mixture is cool; then chill.

Blancmange Pudding

A British dessert, cool and soothing on hot days or after spicy foods.
6-8 servings.

INGREDIENTS:
1/3 cup (75g) sugar
3 Tbsp. cornstarch
2-1/4 cups (650 ml) hot milk
1 tsp. vanilla

METHOD:
Mix the sugar and cornstarch in a saucepan and add 1/4 cup of milk, mixing fast to avoid lumps. Gradually add remaining 2 cups of milk until smooth. Boil for about 7 minutes, constantly stirring. Remove from the heat. Stir in the vanilla. Pour into individual ramekins to cool. Refrigerate for at least 2 hours before serving. Cover well to keep a skin from forming on the top of the blancmange.

.

❧ *It Takes a Village*

Bombay was my village. I walked to all the places that made up my life: the Back Bay Baths, where I swam almost every evening; the Eros and the Regal cinemas, where I fell in love with John Payne and pretended I was Betty Grable or Yvonne De Carlo; the Maccabi and Habonim clubs, where we sang and danced and reaffirmed our love for and connection to our strong Jewish roots; the Keneseth Eliyahu Synagogue, where I chose to follow my spiritual path; my aunts Rae, Rosie, Sophie, and Vicki, who all loved and cherished me; the Convent School, where the nuns gave me a run for my money, pushing me to reach my potential.

I was always in trouble at the Convent. It all started in kindergarten when I felt picked on by Miss Short. Singling me out for talking too much (although we all talked constantly), she made me go up to the front of the classroom with my ruler, then hit me hard on the palm of my hand with it. The ruler broke and I used that as an excuse to show my anger. "I'm going to Mother Superior to report you and put you in jail if you don't give me back a new ruler." I went to Mother Superior, crying miserably, and Mother Superior agreed that I could go home for the rest of the day. Years later, I made a visit to Mother Superior and she said, "Well, I always knew you would turn out to be a lady."

All the parks where we played and the football stadium where we rooted for our special teams were across from our flat. I could walk to Rhythm House, where jazz became my interior melody. Marine Drive was another walking destination and the choice of lovers. It was also the street where Nargis, a well-known Indian actress, lived. She was a good friend of my mother and used our flat as a rendezvous meeting place with Raj Kapoor, another Indian film star, who would meet her at Firuz Ara. All on the quiet because her mother didn't approve, but everyone in Bombay knew that something was going on.

Auntie Chichani and Uncle Ezra

One of the important people in my village was Aunt Chichani, Uncle Ezra Ephraim's wife. Her real name was Simha, but our family changed it to something close to *Chachi*, the Indian word for aunt. She was known as Chichani after that. Although they were wealthy and in good health, she and Uncle Ezra were not lucky with their dream of a family. Chichani gave birth to three boys and three girls and all of them died young. Auntie Chichani never showed her sorrow that I recall and seemed totally engaged in life. She was constantly visiting the homes of her nieces and nephews, perhaps to fill her loss.

My mother was 12 when she became an orphan. She, and her sister, Rose, went to live with Chichani and Uncle Ezra, who loved them as if they were their own children. Thanks to Chichani both sisters became superb cooks of Iraqi food, and both met their future husbands while they lived with their adopted parents. One evening, my father happened to be visiting Aunt Rae, who lived one balcony away from Chichani. Rae and my mother were talking to each other, balcony to balcony, and Dad asked Rae who she was. "My sister," Rae replied. As Mum tells the story over and over again, he was determined to meet her. He walked over to her place, knocked on the door, and when Mum answered, he said, "I want to know you better." He persisted in coming to visit her and finally asked Uncle Ezra for her hand in marriage. When Ezra offered Dad a dowry of Rs.25,000 (a great deal of money in 1932), Dad refused it even though he was poor. One can only imagine how this endeared him to Ezra and Chichani. A few months later Dad was hired by the E.D. Sassoon Mills (EDSU) and a wedding was planned with Dad's parents. Chichani traveled with my mother to Calcutta to meet Meyer and Hannah Sofaer and to marry their son, David Meyer Sofaer, to Mozelle Ephraim Ezekiel.

Dad quickly became one of the top executives for EDSU and on one of his business trips in northern India he had an unusual adventure. He was staying in a boarding house bungalow with a veranda that he enjoyed at the start and end of each day. One very hot day when he returned from work, he went up to the roof of the building to cool off and noticed monkeys and some baboons swinging, via his veranda, from one tree to another. He watched for a while until a very large baboon landed on his veranda. Without thinking, Dad took a brick from the roof and threw it at the baboon, hitting it. The baboon cried out, he said, and jumped up and down "just like a human being."

Within minutes, the trees surrounding the house were full of monkeys and baboons. Dad made a dash for it, racing into his room, locking the door to the staircase on the way. Then he locked his door and the windows. Now he was a prisoner and in deep trouble with the baboons. According to the people in the house, they were out for blood.

Dad stayed inside for over two days with the monkeys and baboons carrying on around the compound.

Eventually an escape plan was hatched. Dad was dressed as a woman and taken by hand carriers in a closed and locked palanquin to the railroad station for a train back to Bombay. The baboons picked up his scent, and no sooner was he locked in a private carriage than a horde of monkeys and baboons arrived at the station as the train pulled out. It always amused me that all he could recall with deep fascination whenever he told this story was that the baboon he had hit sounded "just like a human being."

Chichani was a stern-looking woman who was full of heart for my mother. She often came to see us in a *gaary*, a horse-drawn carriage very much like the those one sees around Central Park. These carriages came to India under the influence of the British Raj and we loved riding in them. My brothers argued over who would get to sit next to the *gaary wala* (the carriage driver), whom they would cajole to give them the reins. During World War II American GIs were seen racing *gaarys* through the streets of Bombay with the laughing driver beside them. I am sure a lot of *baksheesh* (bribes) crossed hands.

Chichani came with lots of sweets and with money jingling in the pockets of her *lapaar*. We were always in a high state of excitement anticipating the many gifts she would bring us. My memory of Chichani is that she smiled easily, seemed to adore each one of us, and was very straightforward in her assessment of situations. When she had dispensed her presents, she and Mum would huddle together to talk.

Her spacious flat in the Nagpada area of Bombay, had a veranda overlooking the field where Auntie Rosie's sons flew kites. They were experts at the popular game of "Patang Baazi," which involves running fine glass on the strings of kites and cutting down the kites of other players. There were constant screams from the field from winners and losers alike. The first time Mum took me to visit Auntie Chichani, I was taken aback by the sight of her and her women friends out on the veranda in the early evening sharing a *nargila* (hookah or water pipe) that my mother later reported contained tobacco and sometimes a small amount of opium. (My mother told me she filled the hookah's container as a child. According to her, her father's older brothers and their wives smoked a small amount of opium in their hookahs from time to time, swearing that their 2% formula kept them healthy.)

Grandpa and Granny

The women on the veranda could have been in Iraq. They were all dressed in *lapaars* with brightly colored, heavily embroidered Spanish shawls draped over their shoulders and the balcony was saturated with the gusty sounds of Arabic. They gossiped about anyone who passed by. It all appeared perfectly harmless until I realized that if you happened to be walking below the veranda while they were at it, you became the subject of discussion. If, heaven forbid, you were a single woman over the age of 21, there was speculation as to what was wrong with you, your family and your "past," followed by suggestions as to which of the available men, well over the age of 50, would be willing to take you as a wife.

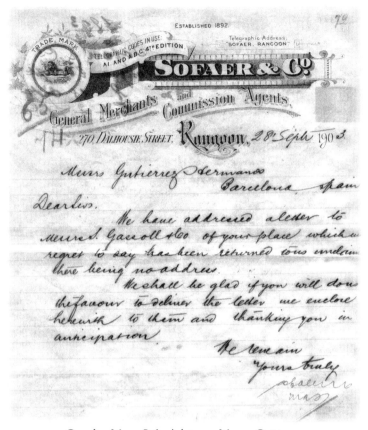

Grandpa Meyer Sofaer's letter to Messrs. Guitierrez
Hermanos in Barcelona, Spain

We also visited Granny and Grandpa, my father's parents. Grandpa always wore soft cotton trousers that looked like pajamas with a loose cotton shirt over them. These clothes originated in Baghdad, and Grandpa and other members of the family continued to wear them in Rangoon and Bombay. With bright blue eyes, a thick head of white hair, and a winning smile, I could understand my Granny's delight in him. He always seemed serious and seldom talked to anyone, as my cousin Effry says, "Grandfather was very aloof. We were very much in awe of him. We could not just open conversations with him. We'd only speak to him when spoken to." He was usually found in his small office, sometimes with his son, Uncle Sonny, who worked with him on the remnants of their huge business from Rangoon.

One of the few conversations I ever had with Grandpa took place in 1948 when we returned to India from England and America. He asked me what I had eaten in boarding school and whether we ate meat. I told him the meat was usually unappetizing gristle that they called stew. He replied that he had been around the world three times by ship; that each journey had taken over nine months; and that he remained kosher during the trips. Then, to make me feel better, he told me that it was not a sin to eat non-kosher meat in order to stay alive.

After my Senior Cambridge exams, Grandpa asked me how they had gone. "They were hard," I remember saying. He looked at me sadly with his bright blue eyes and solemnly said, "Pearl, exams are not hard, they are difficult. Rocks are hard." He always spoke quietly when he wanted to make a point. Our education was important to him and he was constantly available to all the grandchildren whenever we came and asked for school materials. Then he would take us into a storage room that had been converted into a warehouse. There were narrow pathways between stacks of shelves that housed paper of all kinds, glue (I recall he represented LePage), pens and pencils, erasers, crayons, etc.

He advised me never to discuss religion, politics, or money with anyone. Unfortunately my keen concerns regarding the world situation have encouraged me to speak out. I hope he's not saying, "I told her not to talk about politics." But I have been able to follow his advice about money. My father never asked people what they did unless they offered personal information on their own. It felt like an invasion of privacy and both Dad and I have abided by this rule of Grandpa's.

If one of his grandchildren misbehaved, Grandpa would walk around the house asking, "Where is the mother of this child?" He would not tolerate the use of cigarettes, and my parents and aunts and uncles would smoke out of his sight behind closed doors. I recall Auntie Rae and Uncle Sonny's room as the designated "smoker." I don't know how they could breathe in there. Grandpa would also search around for Granny and we often heard his refrain of "Hannah, where are you?" Granny would show up with a sweet smile as if she were a young girl out on her first date. They spoke to each other in Arabic so most of us never knew what they were saying. For years, my parents followed this practice, and Arabic became their secret language when they spoke about the children.

My grandmother Hannah and Grandpa adored each other. I remember that during family celebrations at their home on Sobani Road they would disappear into their bedroom for one or two hours and then reappear flushed and happy. Granny was a tiny woman and wore long skirts and fitted blouses in interesting cotton prints, like Burmese women. She rolled her long hair into a bun that she secured with long tortoise shell pins that stuck up from her head. I always noticed how thin her gold bangles were from her constant busyness. All the keys to all the cupboards and rooms dangled on a ring from her skirt. As my cousin Effry puts it, "She knew what key was for what and she looked after everything and managed that household wonderfully." It was a large household that included Sonny, his wife Rachel and their five children; Aunt Seemah, her husband George and their two children; Uncle Sass and Aunt Girlie and their two daughters, Florence and Becky; Uncle Moses; and occasionally Effry and Edmond during their holidays. Aunt Ramah and her daughter, Irene, lived next door.

With their enormous brood of big eaters, Granny would hide delicacies in a locked *cuppayra*, a small wooden cupboard with netted doors that kept fruit and pastries cool. She would take me to it when we visited and say, "Come, come," and give me something sweet. We played a card game named *chanees*, a child's game she taught me that I, in turn, have taught my children. We sat on the veranda at a white rattan set of furniture that looked out onto the garden and Sobani Road. Although Granny spoke only Hindi and Arabic and since I did not speak Arabic, we had plenty to say to each other in Hindi. My granny was very childlike. She had no formal education and yet she had a sweetness about her that always made me feel welcome and important. She had a special bond with her husband, who, although very sophisticated and a three-time world traveler, still was totally fascinated by this woman.

After Grandpa died, Auntie Seemah and her family moved to London with cousin Iris and Granny. Rachel and her children also moved to London and Uncle Sonny followed after closing up the flat. When I visited London in the summer of 1969 Granny seemed to have adjusted to her new life and proudly showed me her beautiful roses which she tended with a quiet passion. Perhaps my daughter

Ruth has inherited her love for flowers and lust for her garden from her great-grandmother Hannah.

Auntie Rae

All of my mother's five sisters left their imprint on me. Vicki, for her brains and wit; Rae for her fast, objective mind and her trust in me to run her dress store in Poona. I was constantly impressed that Aunt Rae, who had no children of her own, ended up taking full care of Isaac, Auntie Rosie's son, and June, Auntie Sophie's daughter. And she impressed me no end when she told me how she dealt with dirty dishes while living at the Essex House in 1948. Auntie Rae refused to wash dishes. She loved to cook but cleaning up was not part of her vocabulary. She picked up cheap dishware at Woolworth's and after each meal tossed all the dirty plates and cups into the garbage chute on their floor at the Essex House. I learned about style and fashion from Aunt Rae and it always amused me that the American wives of executives in Bombay would insist on getting their clothes through a Ward's catalog rather than having them custom-made in beautiful fabrics by local designers.

I also admired Aunt Rebecca a great deal. She had a beautiful and open face with twinkling eyes and a fast smile. Working in the news and printing business, she managed to support herself and her two children, Simmy and Cecil. She was not divorced, as I think at that time it would have been most difficult for her to get one, but was separated and for years, had a boyfriend, who was usually at her place when we visited. She lived in a small, welcoming house within the confines of a garden full of flowers on Malabar Hill overlooking Chowpatty Beach in Bombay. Her independent and optimistic lifestyle in the setting she had created became a role model for me, as her hopes in life and her aesthetics were close to my own. Her kitchen was plain and primitive. It lacked counters or cabinets and had a concrete floor with a drain in it. Still, the minute you came in the house you knew something yummy was waiting your arrival. She had very few possessions in her very simple house. She always looked happy.

But I was closest to Aunt Soph. I remember her laughter, the gaary rides and movies, the trips to Chowpatty Beach for *malai* (cream) coconuts and *belbal*, the fun in Poona, and the jazz! I remember the trips to Rhythm House and the 78s we bought by Billie Holiday, Fats Waller and Hoagy Carmichael. We played the records on our Philips gramophone, which had great sound, and danced the jitterbug. I can still hear Aunt Soph's jazz piano and voice. When I saw her in Sydney she played by ear every day and entertained us all with her one-liners. (According to my cousin Liza, Aunt Soph referred to Liza's children, Ari and Karen, as "the wild and the mild.") She is no longer with us but her influence on me remains. She played piano until she could no longer sit up.

Our G.I. Joe

Uncle Joe was my mother's younger brother, who joined Uncle Jack in New York after he graduated high school at the age of 16. He met Jack in Paris and they both sailed across a rocky Atlantic Ocean on the

SS *Queen Mary*, arriving in New York City on May 24, 1937. According
to Joe, Jack insisted that he "become Americanized" and sent him
to Columbia University to study languages. Within a couple of years
he was drafted and became a "G.I. Joe." After 13 weeks of training
he sailed out of Fort Mason in San Francisco to Honolulu, Hawaii.
Joe was soon sent to regimental headquarters (because, he said, of his
brains), where the regiment newspaper asked what the United States
Army meant to him as a British subject. "In my love for this country,
which began in the geography class in Bombay, I gave my opinion and
I began to tell them how things out there were and what to anticipate,
almost like warning them that something was gonna happen to this
island." Joe had met an American who had just returned from a tour
of the Far East. "The man said, 'Within two weeks you're gonna hear
from the Japanese.' Nobody paid attention to him. And after Churchill
and Roosevelt met in the middle of the Atlantic Ocean and created
the Atlantic Charter, Hawaii heard from Japan."

Joe recalled December 7, 1941, as his "baptism by fire - a day of
reckoning with things and events undreamed of." He found himself in
the middle of war as a British subject fighting for America, although
within nine months Congress granted all servicemen of foreign birth full
U.S. citizenship. Joe felt that America could have turned things around
against the Japanese very quickly. He could not understand why the
aircraft carriers in the area had been sent to Guam and other bases. He
told me that a week before the bombing, there were small Nippon planes
flying over Oahu taking pictures and when people on the base wanted
to shoot them down they were told, "No, no, no, let them take all the
pictures they want - we'll get back to them when we're good and ready."
The weekend of Pearl Harbor's bombing Uncle Joe had a weekend pass
in Oahu and came home about 2:30am on December 7, 1941.

Joe described that day as follows.

*"7:30am all hell broke loose. We still couldn't believe it. They were
flying overhead and we thought it was aircraft having practice, Sunday
morning practice. A Sergeant from the First World War, boy did he use
juicy words. 'You so and so, are you so blind, don't you see the red ball
of Japan?' Oh my God. You know what? When you see that you don't
know how you feel anymore. You die within you and you don't wanna*

look. What? What, is this real? Can't be, it's fantasy. And you have to go and see if we can get our guns in order because we're an anti-aircraft outfit. Meantime the Japanese had a field day attacking. Two of our guys went into the air and shot down two Japanese planes and came back without being able to land; their planes were broken. And yet they came and said 'Duck Soup' [American slang meaning "a piece of cake" or something that's easy to do].

It was devastating when Pearl Harbor came. You know they had not one wave, they had two, three waves. The Japanese. But then we didn't have any opposition. Can you imagine if we had an aircraft carrier it would be different? We could have gotten up and shot most of them down. And, so many lives would have been [saved] but, we were going to have a war. Courtesy of Mr. Churchill and agreement with Mr. Franklin D. Roosevelt."

Uncle Joe was fortunate to escape the onslaught in the Pacific. Because of his "brains" the U.S. Army sent him first to Stanford University to study Chinese and Far Eastern Studies for a year. Then he went to the Georgetown University State Department School. He joined the O.S.S. and was told that they had a job for him in India. The O.S.S. wanted Joe to locate people in Calcutta who sided with Japan, as Japan was close to invading India through Calcutta. He landed in India on V-E Day and that was when his family heard from him again after a two-year silence. "I'm looking at the key signs and while people are celebrating victory in Europe, I was thinking good lord our job is half done. We still have the sons of Nippon to pay back with a little interest. Who'd ever imagine that we could get to be allies."

Uncle Joe never spoke any more about his O.S.S. work as it was understood that no one talks. During the Cold War the O.S.S. (CIA) had a meeting in a Manhattan hotel to honor surviving veterans of World War II. There was an open bar and they tried to get everyone drunk to see how much each person could drink and still keep his mouth shut. These members were wanted back in Washington but Uncle Joe excused himself as he had a wife and children. World War II left him with disdain for war and when I had dinner with him once on December 7, he cried as he told me how many of his friends died in front of him at Pearl Harbor.

Sign of shop

Uncle Joe had memories of his father and the small shop in Bhindhi Bazaar where Grandfather Ephraim sold fez caps, amber beads, and other religious items for the Muslim population. Grandpa did very well and the business really soared when my mother was born, so they called her *Mazal Tov*. The ready-made caps came from Czechoslovakia in boxes and were assembled in Bombay. The packed boxes were shipped all over India and to Africa. All agreements were word of mouth. Jewish merchants like Grandfather mingled freely with Muslims on the street and no one ever broke their word in business. Joe went to his father's shop many times in their carriage, sitting on his father's lap, and told us that these were some of his sweetest memories of being with his dad.

Kerbah from Grandfather Ephraim's shop

When Grandfather Ephraim became sick with throat cancer brought on by his heavy smoking, Jacob took over the business and was still running it when I visited in 1969. Uncle Jacob gave me a fine necklace of *kerbah* (amber) and taught me to rub amber to check its quality. "If it smells of soap, then it is good quality." Joe remembered how he and Mozelle, my mother, would sit with their father on the veranda when Ephraim was very sick. The two children took their father to the doctor at least three times a week but the cancer proved incurable.

Mozelle and Joe, teenagers in Bombay

One Friday evening, Joe recalled,

> "My father looked at us, gathered Mozelle and me, and said,
> 'You will not see me after tomorrow. Call all the children and my
> brothers.' All the brothers came over the next day with the members
> of the family. They sat on mattresses on the veranda and Ephraim
> and his brothers spoke to one another in Arabic, Farsi and Turkish.
> Ephraim looked at his children, so many, he blessed them all and
> then said, 'You know I have two other sons ... in Iraq.' They brought
> him a photograph of David and Jack and he kissed the photo. He lay
> down on the mattress and very soon after that he died. The next day
> they buried him in the Jewish cemetery and walked miles carrying
> him to the cemetery."

Uncle Joe and Aunt Florrie's children Joy and Camille lost their
mother and their sister Pearl in 2004 and their father in 2006 but
can still laugh and tell a funny story. One of their favorite family
anecdotes is about their "burglar cat Mel," who they finally figured
out had stolen all their missing jewelry. One day, during a spring
cleaning, they found most of their jewels, stuffed into his favorite
couch. Joy lives in New York while Camille lives and teaches art in
Connecticut. Camille is an excellent artist and her sculpture would
look proud in any collection. Joy's eloquence stunned those at Joe's
funeral when she gave a short speech about her father. We all miss
Uncle Joe.

ೞ Thespians

Whenever my cousin Chun-Chun came to visit us in San Francisco, she carried a personal stash of Indian spices. She usually had *haldi* (turmeric), *chili leaves*, *jeera*, (cumin), and various others to cook her famous *Biryani*. As soon as she arrived she would say, "Come on, Come on, I'm dying for some real food. I must cook. Let's go." She would insist on going to the market as soon as possible and invariably we ended up having enough food for at least 20 people. Chun-Chun loved parties and we had a string of them when she was around. Everyone loved her cooking and I was fortunate enough to eat her food in Bombay, London, New York and San Francisco.

Chun-Chun on Teachers Day at the Taj

Her creativity moved from the kitchen and on to the stage. This was a gal who could only see a movie after reading the original book or play. Her passion for the theater started at a very young age. Her mother's insistence on "read before you can go" only made her a more intelligent and brilliant actress. She starred in the BBC's *Staying On* by Paul Scott with Saeed Jaffrey, Trevor Howard and Celia Johnson; in the 1980s she represented India as the primary actor at the Edinburgh Festival; and, besides *Kama Sutra*, her Bollywood performances included *Khatta Meetha* and *Baton Baton Mein*. There were over 4,000 people at her funeral, many of them her former drama students from the schools in Bombay.

Chun-Chun got me involved in theater and music at a very young age. My first chorale was Handel's *Messiah* and my initiation into theater was *The Mad Woman of Chaillot*. She included me in a lot of fun adventures, including picnics at Juhu Beach, cast parties, singing at the drop of a hat no matter where we were, and picking breadfruit off the trees while walking to the Convent School together. I asked her once, "Why don't you stay in the States and become a star?" Chun-Chun laughed and replied, "In America I'm a small fish in a big pond. In India I'm a big fish in a small pond. I want to be a big fish."

Lulu, Pearl and Chun-Chun - three Pearls at the Cricket Club, Bombay

I saw her perform *Antigone* in Bombay. In a soliloquy that lasted well over an hour she went from her full height of 4'9" to 6' tall. Her second husband, Alyque Padamsee, an actor of special fame (he was Jinnah in the film *Gandhi*), knew Chun-Chun's strengths. I remember he called her "Pixie," knowing full well she was anything but.

She remained careful about her celebrity and told her children, "No matter what happens; no matter what is written about you, never believe a word of it. If you believe the good things critics say about you, you have to believe the bad." Her children, Raell and Ranjit, have been able to stay grounded even though people recognize them wherever they go in Bombay and ask for autographs. Ranjit says, "When I moved to Canada I wrote a letter to her. On the envelope I wrote 'Pearl Padamsee, Bombay, India.' I didn't write any address. And it got to her. That's the extent of her tentacles." When her mother did *Khatta Meetha*, Raell says the two of them couldn't go anywhere in Bombay without being stopped. And, because of Chun-Chun's disregard for all the paraphernalia that can come with fame, both Raell and Ranjit live simple lives and are not overawed by celebrity.

Ranjit in Such A Long Journey

Raell and Ranjit have been strongly influenced by Chun-Chun's love of theater and have both followed in her footsteps. Ranjit describes himself as "a work in transit." He began theater in his school years and quickly formed *Stages*, a group that performed one-act plays throughout India. He has acted in Bollywood, in Canada, and in Hollywood, where he has had roles in TV's *NYPD Blue*, *The Cosby Show*, *Law & Order*, and in *Mississippi Masala* with Denzel Washington, Spike Lee's *Girl 6*, and, the most recent with Queen Latifah and LL Cool J in *Last Holiday*. He said he learned an important lesson from Bill Cosby, whom he describes as an "absolute genius:" "I learned not to be scared. Comedians can't be scared; you just have to be prepared to make a fool of yourself."

He has been in a long list of other films and is currently writing an animated television series called *Animal Times* plus a feature film *If It Ain't Halal...It Ain't Kosher*. Ranjit's most exquisite work, from his point of view, is caring for his son, Avishay, who Ranjit feels is his new boss. And to both Ranjit and his wife, Malini, it is important for Avi to know both the cultures he has inherited. As Ranjit puts it, "After all, he is an Indian American."

Poonam, Raell and Boman – children in performance

While Ranjit has adopted New York City as his home, Raell lives in Bombay, where she has started over 16 children's theater workshops that will eventually go national. Raell's most important activity is bringing under-privileged children, children from middle-class and upper-class homes, and children from challenged backgrounds to perform together in the workshops. She hopes to make a film of this work within the year. She has had her own office equipment business since the age of 19 and tells me she manages many of the Padamsee family's properties. Even with her countless responsibilities she exudes a calm that draws people to her.

The family's flat in Belha Terrace was Ranjit and Raell's first theater. The drawing room was the stage, the bedrooms the exits. The audience sat on the terrace and could watch the actors through the large open space that usually housed glass doors. In addition to performances at Belha Terrace, there were workshops, impromptu dinners for thirty to forty people each day, and a form of group therapy where everyone helped one another solve their problems. Raell and Ranjit describe their home as warm and vibrant, but they were aware that their mother had many surrogate children, including her students of drama and elocution at five different schools in Bombay. Chun-Chun taught them, directed them, fed them, and gave them a shoulder to cry on.

Both Raell and Ranjit have very fond memories of their grandmother "Nani Vicki." Ranjit remembers going with her to the race course and to the synagogue, where she would always meet her neighbor Harry Sopher. Ranjit says, "She and Harry Sopher would talk horses in both places and I got to thinking the synagogue was an indoor race track. I was about 6 years old, mind you." He also says that "for years I thought my name was *mamzer* and that everything was named *aku-si-yat*." Ranjit, in his naivete had no idea his grandmother was calling him a bastard and no good. To Aunt Vicki's credit, she used these Arabic expressions as endearments, as none of us ever heard her speak that way.

Besides their confusion about the various languages they heard from their Nani, Raell and Ranjit were confused about their religion and heritage. Most people in India are identified by religion and language. Their maternal grandfather, Althaf Amber, was a Muslim

who converted to Christianity. Their maternal grandmother, Victoria
Ezekiel, was a Jew. Ranjit's father was a Hindu and his stepfather and
Raell's father, Alyque Padamsee was a converted Hindu and is now a
Muslim. Their mother was considered a Jew by Vicki and a Christian
by Althaf and when Raell asked her nani, "But what am I?" Vicki said,
"I am Jewish so your mother is Jewish and now you are Jewish.' Raell
was confused when Aunt Rebecca would come over with her own set
of *hundis* (cooking vessels) to make her own kosher food. Raell didn't
even know what *kosher* meant.

Both Auntie Vicki and Uncle Althaf were brilliant, so Chun-Chun
had to work hard to keep up with the family fame. Both were highly
independent thinkers, which meant frequent fighting matches. Raell
and Ranjit often found themselves in the middle of a small war, as did
their mother. Vicki and Althaf were intellectuals who kept in touch
with the immediate family but also knew what was happening in the
rest of the world. I remember Aunt Vicki describing Kew Gardens in
London to me after I returned from England. With her passion for
knowledge, she knew about places she had never been.

Vicki worked as head secretary for the American oil company
Caltex throughout the Middle East. She was highly respected and
her bosses freely admitted that Mrs. Vicki Waiz "ran the company."
When she retired, besides playing cards, she worked hard to create
and support refuges for the many magnificent animals that were being
destroyed by "sportsmen." The Bengal tiger and the exquisite white
tiger are awesome to watch, and if you are ever in India, do visit local
zoos to see them. My first sight of white tigers was at the Delhi zoo
and they moved me to tears with their powerful beauty.

Uncle Althaf was deeply involved in the Congress party from the
time both he, and Mahatma Gandhi, lived in South Africa. Althaf's
book, *Indians in South Africa*, depicted the prejudice against the Indian
community and he worked with Gandhi in his creation of a *Satyagraha*
stance in South Africa. Satyagraha, which in ancient Sanskrit means
the effort to apply truth, was the basis of the philosophy of non-
violence as practiced by Mahandas Gandhi: in South Africa against
apartheid and in India to bring to an end the rule of the British Raj.
Uncle Althaf worked doggedly, as did many others, to obtain freedom
from British rule and, when that eventually came about, he served as

the Indian ambassador to Fiji for two years. When he and his family returned to India he offered me a shrunken head from Fiji, but I politely refused.

ೞ *Mom's Chicken Biryani*

Serves 10-12

INGREDIENTS:
2 chickens skinned & cut into pieces
1 cup (3kg) plain yogurt
4oz cut-up ginger
4oz crushed garlic
1 tsp. saffron
1 tsp. cumin
1 tsp. cardamom
3-4 sticks cinnamon
12 chopped medium size chilies
1/2 tsp. black pepper
1 lb. 3 oz (1/2 kg) basmati rice
2 lbs. 3 oz (1 kg) potatoes, cleaned & cut into small pieces
2 lbs. 3 oz (1 kg) yellow onions cut fine & long
1 cup (300 ml) olive oil

METHOD:
Add yogurt to the chicken and mix well, grind all spices into a masala (paste), salt to taste; partially brown the chicken in it's fat; add all spices and yogurt and marinate the whole night.

Deep-fry the cut potatoes until golden brown, fry cut onions until golden brown.

Parboil rice with salt to taste, until 3/4 of the water has gone and rice is still wet.

In a flat, deep pot, lay down 1/3 of the rice, add half the cooked chicken; cover with another layer of rice (1/3 of original); cover with cooked potatoes and onion; then a layer of chicken. Continue with layers until top layer is rice.

Heat the oil and pour all over the rice. Cover the pot and cook on low for 1 hour. Move to pre-heated oven at 300°F (150°C) for 1 more hour. Serve hot.

ℂℨ *Khatta Meetha Dahl*

(sweet and sour lentils)
A side dish that serves 10-12.

INGREDIENTS:
1/2 lb. (1/4 kg) dahl (lentils)
4 small red chilies, chopped
1/4 tsp. ground black pepper
1/2 tsp. ground cloves
1/2 tsp. ground cardamom
4 cloves garlic, peeled and smashed
1 Tbsp. ginger, peeled and chopped
1 Tbsp. cumin
salt to taste
1/2 cup olive oil
1/8 cup (28 gm) brown sugar
1 oz (28 gm) tamarind (available crushed in small bottles)

METHOD:
Boil the dahl in a small stock pot with 4 cups (940 ml) of water. Continuously remove scum from the surface of the water. Cook until dahl is soft, then strain.

In a separate, medium cooking pot, with cover, brown the chilies, pepper, cloves, cardamom, garlic and ginger in the olive oil. Simmer, covered, for 15 minutes.

In a 1/4 cup (60 ml) of water, mix brown sugar and tamarind.

Add the strained dahl to the spice mixture plus 1 cup (240 ml) water and bring to boil. Add sugar mixture and salt to taste. Mix well and simmer about 1/2 to 1 hour, until dahl becomes soupy. Be sure the dahl is cooked long enough so that it is not watery. This is a good side dish with curry and rice.

ೞ *Linguine with Spicy Thai Fish Sauce*

Serves 4-6

INGREDIENTS:
12 oz (340 gm) linguine, uncooked
12 oz (340 gm) cubed red snapper, or fish of your choice
3 red bell peppers, seeds and stems removed, cut into bite-size,
thin strips
3 scallions, thinly sliced (white part and tips of green part)
2 tsp. smooth peanut butter
1 Tbsp. sesame oil
1/2 cup (120 ml) low-sodium chicken broth or water
1/2 tsp. (2 ml) crushed red pepper flakes
1 jalapeno pepper, stemmed, seeded, and thinly sliced
1/2 tsp. ground ginger
1 Tbsp. low sodium-soy sauce
1 Tbsp. mild white vinegar

METHOD:
Prepare linguine according to package directions. While noodles are cooking,
combine remaining ingredients in a saucepan and place over low heat. Cover
and simmer until the sauce is smooth and the fish is cooked through, about
5 to 10 minutes.

When linguine is done, drain well and transfer to large serving bowl. Add
sauce and toss gently until well combined. Serve immediately.

The Evil Eye and Other Strange Happenings

Belief in superstitions, and principally in *ayn ha'ra*, or the evil eye, was a major underpinning in our lives. Every year at Rosh Hashanah, my parents would follow the age-old practice of *kapparah*, which was designed to ward off the evil eye. A live hen or rooster, depending on our gender, would be swung around each of our heads as the person swinging the chicken prayed over us. Basically, the idea was that the poor creature would receive any sickness or negative energy that might be festering in our bodies. The spiritually compromised bird would then be given to feed poor people. This practice totally appalled me. As a child I was terrified of it and covered my ears, head down, to shut out the shrieking of the birds. As I grew older, I considered that we were engaged in a well-meaning, perhaps, but mean-spirited tradition. I felt ashamed to pass on my ailments, even symbolically, to poor people. I hated the whole routine and complained bitterly every year, which definitely got me into trouble. Why was this a religious thing to do? Weren't we passing on not only our sicknesses but also the curse of the evil eye itself?

The protests of one child, of course, were no match for the evil eye, which ruled over us and our people. Throughout the Middle East people still wear turquoise to ward off the evil eye, which is seen principally as jealousy that has the power to harm a person's well-being, both mentally and physically. Among the Iraqi Jews of Bombay, people avoided idle talk of success or beauty; comments like "Business is good" or "You look lovely." People were jealous of one another, especially of others' success. It was much safer not to talk about one's success and have the evil eye, symbolically, spit on you. As I grew older I realized that fear of the evil eye was probably why I had never received a compliment from any of my elder family members. Little did they know how much I needed to hear a good word or receive a loving touch. Now as an adult, I am always telling my children and grandchildren how terrific they are.

Many of the rituals we practiced related to our Jewish festivals. We went to synagogue on Tisha Ba'av, the day of mourning that commemorates the destruction of the First and Second Temples in Jerusalem. Everything in the synagogue was covered in black and the prayers were sad and plaintive. Many people cried as they mourned personal losses. After the service my mother would take us shopping and buy each of us something new to wear that day to cast away the sadness we may have taken in. She would also buy fabric, always white, for new clothes to be made for Rosh Hashanah and Yom Kippur.

Culturally, the evil eye, or "coveting," was taken very seriously not only among us Jews but among the Muslim and Hindus in India as well. If you admired a possession of someone's and remarked on it emphatically, you would inevitably be offered the item by the owner, who would assume that if your admiration was that great it was best to let it go as otherwise it would never bring him or her pleasure or good health. I quickly learned never to admire another's possessions.

Dreams had a strong influence on our daily lives. If you dreamt of a dead parent it was a "sign" and you would *fast* in order to receive clearer messages. Often a dream resulted in charity because the dream foretold a disaster. Or we gave charity in thanks because the dream's message was a marriage or the birth of a much wanted child. We had a Hebrew teacher whom we called "Master Abey." He had a wonderful voice and I still chant *Tehillim* (Psalms) as he taught me. Master Abey became a close friend and I shared many of my problems with him, including my dreams, which he always asked me about. Years later I saw him in London and he told me that my dreams had been a source of income for him. He figured out numbers based on the dreams and would bet the "numbers." These were the open and closing values of cotton on the market each day. Abey sheepishly said, "And I always won." I smiled and said, "Then how come I didn't get a cut?" *Now, I wish I had asked him to teach me how to interpret dreams.*

* * * * * * * * * *

When I was 16, I ran a high fever. Dr. Pereira was summoned but couldn't diagnose my condition. "Nothing is wrong with her," he concluded. My mother was frantic and called her Auntie Hannah. Soon there was a general muttering and carrying on in the kitchen. They brought me in and I saw a lit charcoal *sigree* (brazier) over which Auntie Hannah held a pan. Silently, and without my noticing, she slipped a piece of lead into the pan. Once the lead was melted, she set down a pan of cold water. Then, having touched my head a few times and muttered several *abdaluks* (darling) and other words in Arabic, she poured the molten lead into the cold water. This process, known as *kisas* (lead in Arabic), is enacted whenever there is a problem that seems unsolvable. Through it all I sat quietly as did the others in the household, watching with intense interest. Looking back, I realize that I was quite terrified and in awe of my female elders.

The lead solidified into a shape and was removed from the water. It looked like a tennis racquet. Auntie asked me to recount what I had been up to lately, and when I came to tennis, which I loved, I was directed never to play tennis again, or to be friends with my recent tennis opponent: "She has her evil eye on you and hates you." Within the day, my fever broke. Needless to say, the entire experience left me bewildered and off balance. Could I really believe Auntie Hannah and must I obey her? What would happen if I disobeyed? I was not especially close to my tennis opponent so there was no friendship I would have missed. Years later, when I visited Jerusalem, I met her with mutual friends. She was warm and sincerely happy to see me. She invited me to her home. Her evil eye, I realized, was entirely a product of the imaginative powers of the grownups.

Belief in *kisas* is not limited to the Middle East. Recently, my friend Lisa brought me a gift of metal pieces after a visit to Vienna. The Viennese melt pieces of metal on New Year's Eve and then pour the liquid metal into a pan of cold water. Whatever shape the metal creates is your future for the coming year. When, I wondered, had this superstition crossed the waters of the Mediterranean?

* * * * * * * * * *

Sometimes objects are thought to absorb and negate the effect of the evil eye. When my cousins Effry and Alice had a son, J.J., their friend Helen immediately gave Alice a piece of alum to put in her purse to protect him from the evil eye. Shortly afterward, Alice and J.J. went to the store, where many people admired him. Later that evening, when Alice emptied her purse, she saw the alum piece smashed to smithereens. Helen explained that the alum had broken apart from the effects of the evil eye on J.J. and had stopped all the jealousy and negativity from hurting the child.

Alice has several stories concerning the evil eye. One of her favorites is of a woman she and Effry knew when they lived in Canada. The woman was childless and had only one healthy eye (the other was glass). She loved to visit Alice and particularly liked Alice's daughter Rachel. One day she put her hand on Rachel's head and said, "Why can't I have this one?" Three days later, Rachel's eye, the same one where the woman had a glass eye, went blind. The doctors determined there was swelling in Rachel's optic nerve but said it should not cause blindness. Alice and Effry went to their rabbi who told them to contact a Rabbi Doueck, a cabalist in Los Angeles. When they phoned him, without any prior contact by anyone, he seemed to know all about their family and their problem and said he would help Rachel. Upon his request they sent him Rachel's photo and he sent them a prayer to put over Rachel's bed. He told them that her eye would get worse before it got better.

A couple of days later Rachel could not see with her other eye. The family was alarmed and once again rushed Rachel to the doctors, but they had no answers. Rachel was totally blind. During this time, the glass-eyed woman phoned daily to find out how Rachel was. Finally, a week later, Rachel's eyesight came back and stayed normal from then on. The following year Alice went to visit Rabbi Doueck and he told Alice their family would move from Canada to live in Israel, which they eventually did. He would not accept any money from Alice for helping Rachel.

One of the most beautiful rituals against the evil eye has its roots in the Middle East and is practiced by both Jews and Muslims. It is called *chamsah,* from the Hamitic root meaning five and represents the protective hand of God. To safeguard a bride from jealousy, the bride's fingers and feet are painted with henna by her women friends prior to the wedding night. In India the ritual is followed by Hindus, Jews and Muslims and is known as the *mhendi* ceremony. This tradition has also caught the fancy of many Westerners. When my youngest daughter, Ruth, got married, her closest women friends all happily participated. It delights me that my daughter has continued a tradition that began among our family members in Baghdad.

10

ೞ *Poona*

Every summer we went to Poona on the *Deccan Queen*. The *Queen* was the fastest train in India and it still serves "cheese toast," which I yearn for whenever I remember our trips. It's simple to prepare: toast some bread; cover each piece with the cheese of your choice (mine is white cheddar), and broil until bubbly. If you like, you can spread mustard or another condiment on the toast prior to adding the cheese. Serve with a hot cup of tea. That was our main meal on the *Queen* even though there were vendors selling delicious choices of delectable foods at all the stations along the way. My parents were always concerned we could get sick, so we never got a taste. They took us in a closed compartment, ordered cheese toast and soft drinks for us and of course, tea for them. We never got lost on that train.

After India's independence we were told that the British had left India the finest railroad system in the world. They laid tracks through the jungles between Bombay (Mumbai) and Poona (Pune) and blasted tunnels through the hills of the Western Ghats. We had a game of counting the tunnels, shouting out the number to one another as we went through the hills in a dark void. Most of the tunnels were short so they weren't scary. For the workers on this set of rails, who had to deal with intense heat, mosquitoes, snakes, and tigers, the experience had been grim. Many of them apparently died. I would sit in our protected car and imagine tigers stalking in the jungles we passed through. There are tigers still living there.

Bombay is extremely hot and humid during the summer months and I remember the feeling of anticipation that seemed to rise from the passengers when we got to Lonaavala, the first hill station up to Poona. My mother could not wait to get out of the heat in Bombay and as Dad was enticed by the horse races at the Turf Club in Poona, off we went every summer. And how wonderful it all was. One summer we rented a large Victorian bungalow and had visitors constantly through the season. Dad took the *Deccan Queen* to work every Monday morning and came back every Friday evening. My mother and some of the servants stayed with us and we had the company of many family members, including Aunt Rae and Aunt Sophie, who lived there part-time to run Aunt Rae's dress shop in Poona. One afternoon, Auntie Rae left me in charge of the shop while she went to lunch. I will never forget my first sale – it was an evening gown to an American GI. whom I found quite enchanting. We chatted and he teased me. I stopped blushing when Auntie Rae returned and I handed her R. 260. She was quite surprised and gave me a lot more responsibility after that.

Tonga in Poona

Every day began with breakfast and a shower, then we were off to the Bund Gardens on a *tonga*, a horse-drawn covered rickshaw on high large wheels where the passengers sat with their backs to the driver. We often took sandwiches of wonderful bread made by a well-known European baker in Poona and spread with homemade pot cheese and my grandmother's gooseberry jam. We played in the gardens and cooled off near the small waterfalls throughout the park. Then home for lunch and an afternoon nap. I remember helping my mother make fresh tomato juice under the trees in the garden. In the 1940s there were no "mixers." Our hands had to be strong but the reward was the best tomato juice I've ever tasted. The air, laden with the scents of fresh fruit and flowers, always felt soft and protective in Poona.

Poona had its own sounds and aromas. The crowing of cocks was our alarm clock. When I stayed with friends of mine in Kauai recently, they apologized for the exuberance of the cocks. "Don't worry," I said. "That is the sweet sound of Poona for me." The sounds of trains during the night now seem familiar and nostalgic. But the strange screams of the jackals every night were not friendly and certainly not sounds I want to hear again. The warm sun and light breezes spread the scent of roses everywhere. And when the humid monsoon rains cooled us down, the house developed an appetizing aroma of mangoes, which seemed to be jumping out of the baskets in our kitchen.

My brother Abe related an intriguing adventure that occurred one summer morning in Poona:

> "I remember going down the stairs of the house in which we were staying. We had heard that there was a cobra in the area and that it had killed one or two animals. As I stepped on the bottom step, which was made of wood and had a space between it and the ground, a big king cobra slipped out from under the step and curled up in front of me. I froze. It looked at me and I don't know whether I was hypnotized or simply scared silly, but I just stood there with my arms out screaming. The snake looked at me, leaning to the right and left. Mom was up on the porch and saw what was happening. She screamed and fainted. The boy who worked in the garden saw the situation and a man yelled at him to do something. The boy grabbed an axe and came over to try to kill the snake with it. The man yelled at the boy that he could cut off my leg if he missed. So the boy picked up a bamboo stick and came behind the snake and took a hard swing at it while it was busy looking at me. The stick hit the snake under its

head and knocked off the head and sent it flying into the next yard. I
collapsed. Pretty soon, everyone was making a huge fuss over me and
I remember the British commander in Poona let me come over to the
military station and lead a small group of men in marching back and
forth, which was a blast for me at that age. No one made a big fuss
over the chokra [boy servant] who saved my life, which was a shame,
since he was very skillful and effective."

The cobra was turned over to the Haffkine Institute, an
organization founded in the 1930s that collected samples of snake
venom in order to develop an anti-venom. But our relief turned to
fear when the servants warned us that the cobra's mate would return
for retribution. That night, there were deep discussions and anxious
concerns. None of us slept well. The idea of an unwanted visitor in
the middle of the night put all of us in a restless state. The next day,
the servants reported that a snake had come during the night and
killed the milking cow in the back garden.

Indian villagers are reluctant to kill a snake, fearing such
repercussions. The snake had been sacred in Indian culture before
the arrival of the Aryans from the north and it was worshiped before
the advent of idols and Hinduism. Historically, most peasants looked
upon the snake as a deity, because it ate the rodents in the fields and
protected their harvest. One day every year, the peasants did not work
in their fields but prayed to the snake and provided it with milk and
eggs. The practice is still followed in some villages.

According to legend, a farmer accidentally killed two baby snakes
in his field. The mother snake came to his house the next day and
killed all the occupants except for one daughter, who had been praying
to the snake god that day. Legends have a way of changing through
the years, but perhaps the fear our servants expressed was based on
this tradition.

Today, people who are part of India's *naag* (snake culture) regard
the snake as second only to the cow in sacredness. The king cobra is
associated with the *lingam*, the symbol of fire and healing energy that
moves from the base of the spine to the crown of the head. The snake
is the personification of psychic energy activated through the *chakras*
(seven levels of energy based in the spinal cord); it is also known as

kundalini shakti, which translates literally as "coiling like a snake."

In Poona, we always visited Auntie Sarah, my mother's maternal aunt and Uncle Eddie. Auntie Sarah was fun and gregarious and I remember feeling that it would be wonderful to have a house and a beautiful garden like hers when I grew up. She had dahlias the size of a very large open hand and roses that immersed you in their scent as you walked up a gravel path to the front door of their simple one-story home. Inside there was always the scent of fresh, delicious foods and Auntie Sarah's specialty of sweet *luzina*. Maggie, my mother's cousin, gave me her mom's recipe when I saw her in Tel Aviv.

Inside her house, Auntie Sarah observed an unusual custom. She hung large eggs high up on the walls, attaching them on to nails through a small hole in each egg. It always seemed very strange to see eggs all over the walls in the house but evidently it was a method of keeping lizards out of the house. The lizards lived in the rafters of the roof and the smell of the rotting eggs drove them away. Fortunately, the roof was so high that none of us could smell the eggs. No harmful pesticides - and a most original way to keep unwanted fauna out of one's living areas.

Our Aunt Hannah had her share of superstitions. She also seemed able to foresee the future. Maggie tells me that when she was six years old and happily playing hopscotch, Auntie Hannah told her to stop playing and to listen to what she had to tell her. She told Maggie, "One day you won't need to wash plates by hand; one day, you will press a button and get what you need." She showed Maggie a passage in the Bible that said, "There will come a time ... everything will happen in a split second."

Maggie reminds me of a pillow fight that Abe and I had with her and her brother, Jacob. We broke a pillow, and as the feathers flew around the room, Auntie Sarah and my mother reprimanded us. We were sent outside, but that was no punishment as we had a garden of Uncle Eddies' Model T Fords to play with. Uncle Eddie was my hero. He had an innate knowledge of automobiles, which were his profession. The numerous antique cars in the front yard, Maggie explained to me, were automobiles he had repaired whose various owners had never returned to claim. Uncle Eddie had a fortune's worth of these cars, but as they were not really his and since he was a highly ethical man, the cars were left on the property when the family emigrated to Israel in the 1960s.

Cousins meet in Tel Aviv

My favorite game in Uncle Eddies' yard was to sit on the top seat of a Ford fire engine and pretend I was a fireman on the way to a rescue. In the canary yellow Packard with running boards on the side, I became a divine Hollywood star sitting next to the driver as I had seen Betty Grable and Lana Turner doing in their movies. There was a Daimler, and a Volga, one of the first Russian cars, black and foreboding. One could imagine KGB agents occupying its dismal interior. Jacob told me that his father also had a car named the "Beam," which was so unique that there is a film about it.

Uncle Eddie was a very quiet man. He had a sweet, charming smile and manner that reminds me of his daughter Lulu's husband and cousin, Eddie Abraham, who also worked with automobiles. Uncle Eddie is someone I would have liked to know better. After all, how many people in this world have a collection of Model T Fords, Packards, even a "Beam" sitting in their front yard?

One of the main landmarks for us in Poona was the Ohel David synagogue. This impressive red brick structure was long and narrow, with a clock tower and a 90-foot spire. I was told that the spire kept the synagogue safe from lightning strikes, which we had plenty of during the summer monsoons. The interior had magnificent stained glass windows in colors that lit up the synagogue like a light show.

The Sassoon family, for whom my father worked, had built what we affectionately called the "Poona Synagogue," together with the Magen David Synagogue in Byculla, Bombay and the Keneseth Eliyahu Synagogue in Fort, Bombay, where my family worshiped. These were built between 1860 and 1880 and were the centers of activity for the Jewish communities in Poona and Bombay. David Sassoon, who had a summer home in Poona, was buried on the grounds of the Poona Synagogue in a dignified mausoleum in 1864. His grandson, Jacob Sassoon, built the free Sir Jacob Sassoon High School on the synagogue grounds in Byculla and even had ovens on the grounds where all Passover *matzoth* for the Jewish community were baked. The Fort synagogue, which I attended, held all the Habonim meetings for us and I loved being in the sukkah, (the small temporary arbor, decorated with fresh fruit and vegetables of the harvest), during the Sukkoth holiday.

Habra (welfare) was the foundation of our community. As a child, I remember hearing my mother talk about the "milk fund" at the Sassoon school. We had many financially stable families, but there were also poor people who had little education and, often, very large families to support. Most of the Jewish charities focused on the welfare of the children of these large families. If a poor Jewish family had a newborn, or a wedding, or a death, there were people in our community who rallied around and brought money, food, clothing, whatever was needed, and took care of those Jews in need.

This commitment to *habra* was the underpinning of the Sassoon philosophy. The Sassoon Fund gave poor students scholarships to attend universities around the world. Their emphasis on education was expanded by the Sassoon Library, housed in a beautiful building and appreciated by the entire Bombay community. For newly arrived unschooled Jewish men from Baghdad, they set up taxi cab companies to give them an opportunity for immediate income. Besides the synagogues and school, the Sassoons funded a free cemetery where any Jew could be buried. The family did its best to give back to the community that had created a safe haven for it when David Sassoon came to Bombay as a refugee from Baghdad in 1826.

A most colorful member of the clan was Lady Ezra Sassoon, who lived in Calcutta and was known for her passion for animals – her collection of creatures became her private zoo. She was considered a royal eccentric and much admired for her efforts to save and care for wild creatures. Even in India, she was unusual and exceptional in her dignity and resolve to care for the unusual animals she kept as personal pets. It was my honor to receive a hand-forged silver rattle from her at my birth, and all my children and grandchildren have chewed on that rattle at one time or another. It is now awaiting the teeth of the next Sofaer generation, my great-grand-children.

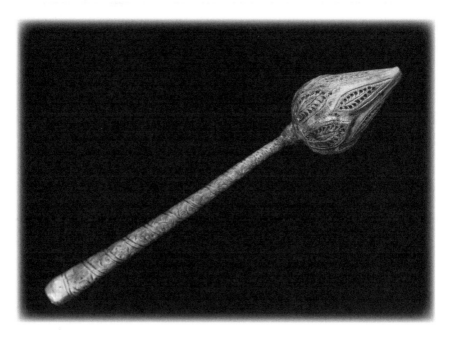

My baby rattle

Errata

❧ *Tiparee (Gooseberry) Jam*

Granny used to make this when gooseberries were in season in the Himalayas. Grandpa would have fresh boxes of gooseberries shipped down to Bombay for Granny's special jam. Uncle Sass shared her simple recipe.

INGREDIENTS:
1 lb. (454 gm) gooseberries
1 lb. sugar*
vanilla or cardamom to taste

METHOD:
Cook down slowly with just enough water to keep from burning. Great on toast.

*Note:
Recipe inadvertently indicated 1 tsp. sugar.
This page corrects amount to 1 lb. sugar.

Errata

🕸 *Tibaree (Gooseberry) Jam*

Granny used to make this when gooseberries were in season in the Himalayas. Grandpa would have fresh boxes of gooseberries shipped down to Bombay for Granny's special jam. Uncle Sass shared her simple recipe.

INGREDIENTS:
1 lb. (454 gm) gooseberries
1 lb. sugar*
vanilla or cardamom to taste

METHOD:
Cook down slowly with just enough water to keep from burning. Great on toast.

*Note:
Recipe inadvertently indicated 1 tsp. sugar.
This page corrects amount to 1 lb. sugar.

❧ *Tiparee (Gooseberry) Jam*

Granny used to make this when gooseberries were in season in the Himalayas. Grandpa would have fresh boxes of gooseberries shipped down to Bombay for Granny's special jam. Uncle Sass shared her simple recipe.

INGREDIENTS:
1 lb. (454 gm) gooseberries
1 tsp. sugar
vanilla or cardamom to taste

METHOD:
Cook down slowly with just enough water to keep from burning. Great on toast.

○ℬ *Luzina*

Wonderful and cool dessert of the Middle East.

INGREDIENTS:
2.2 lbs. (1 kg) shredded coconut
3.3 lbs. (1-1/2 kg) sugar
1-2 tsp. citric acid
4-1/2 8oz glasses water
rosewater, to taste

METHOD:
Mix all ingredients and cook on a low to medium flame until sticky. Pour out onto a flat greased surface (a large baking pan that is 2" deep).

Cool for an hour and then refrigerate. Cut into squares or diamond shapes.

Down Under

Part III

०३ *The Moses Clan*

One of the best parts about going to Crawford Market in Bombay was visiting my cousin, Alfy, the son of Aunt Rosie and Uncle Joe, who ran his father's small shop a block from the market. The shop was like many of the stalls found in the Crawford Market. No one went in to buy. Instead, Alfy brought out items to his customers from the boxes of haberdashery stored on shelves along the interior walls. He would usually sit on a cushion on the floor of the shop that was higher than the footpath. Like the Crawford Market merchants, he would show customers merchandise as they stood on the sidewalk. Alfy started to work in his early teens with what seemed like a very positive sales persona and, although that experience was probably the foundation of his business acumen, I felt he lost out on parts of his childhood. I couldn't help but wonder just how many sales of *singlets* (t-shirts) were needed to support a family of twelve.

They lived in Nagpada, a district in Bombay, in a tiny flat with only two rooms and a small balcony. The logistics of housing two adults and ten children in such a small place must have been more than challenging. The kitchen was outside the flat down a hall, and the residents on the floor shared two bathrooms located at the end of the apartments. Many of the people on the first floor were part of the paternal Moses family so the cousins grew up together. The wives created a strong support system, helping one another during births, deaths, and marriages, their kitchens often humming with communal gossip as they prepared food for these special occasions.

Eating together on Sabbath was so important that the dining table and chairs consumed one of the family's two precious rooms. The long oak table was covered with plates of food creating a mosaic of color that would whet anybody's appetite: red beetroot *hamad*, the golden brown roast chicken surrounded by *aloomakala* (whole fried potatoes), the green *halbah* (relish) plate, the red tomato salad, and the green *bamya* (okra). Auntie Rosie's brass *tiryah*, a candelabra, with nine glass cups for oil, hung over the center of the table. On Sabbath they lit seven; the nine were for Hanukah. The genuine welcome from Auntie Rosie and Uncle Joe was reflected by the warmth and beauty created by the *tiryah*. There were always many others at Sabbath besides family members. Some who had no home and, perhaps, no food, crowded around the table. Everyone was accepted.

Sometimes I was lucky enough to be there on a Friday night and shared my cousin Lulu's bed. I remember the busyness of the kitchen down the hall and Eetoo, their cook, working with Auntie Rosie all day. Auntie Rosie knew that *aloomakala* was my favorite of her dishes and always made it when I came. This is not a low-fat recipe, but oh! what ecstasy. Sometimes, after dinner, Alfy would get me a sweet *pan*, ground beetlenut with spices rolled up in a leaf. You chew it and if you spit it out, as some Indians do, it leaves a red stain. The streets of Bombay have red stains everywhere.

Where did Auntie Rosie get her motivation with ten children to care for? Despite their demands, she always had a peaceful manner. When I stayed there I noticed that Uncle Joe would get up early to boil water for the day, then bring a fresh cup of tea to Auntie Rosie in their bed. This struck me as a reflection of his gentler side and made me understand why my mother always said, "They love each other." Perhaps it also explains Rosie's soft and beautiful face.

She raised a fine brood. Alfy, in particular, has a special place in my heart. He was so kind and patient when he taught me to drive a car. On one of our excursions the look of terror belied the calm in his voice. "Pearl," he said, "you are not supposed to drive on the pavement; you must stay on the street." (Imagine my surprise many years later in Paris when I saw most cars parked on the pavement.) Alfy would come and get me at my school, Walsingham House on Malabar Hill, at lunchtime, and take me out for ice cream. Along with Eze Meyer, who taught me how to ride a bicycle, and Eze's brother Eddie, who made sure I was okay at various outings, Alfy was one of the boy cousins who looked out for me as I grew up in Bombay. I felt totally protected with these guys around.

The Moses clan in Bombay

Although Alfy and his future wife, Molly, grew up in the same area of Bombay, and were both of Baghdadi heritage, they didn't meet until they were in their twenties, when they both attended the prayers of *shivah* (mourning) for our Uncle David after he died en route to Australia. In each of their 10-sibling families, Alfy and Molly were known to be reliable, hard-working, risk takers and leaders. They were attracted to each other right away and community members got together to make a match. Now, they are heading toward a half century of marriage, emphatically devoted to each another. In honor of Uncle David, they named their first child David.

Molly's mother, Miriam, was born to a poor family in Baghdad. There were so many mouths to feed that Miriam's parents sent her to Bombay to live with an aunt and uncle who had no children. Following Baghdadi custom, her aunt and uncle arranged her marriage when she was 14, to Yatta Ya Ezekiel, age 19. The marriage lasted 62 years.

Molly's family, the Ezekiels, moved to Australia with other Baghdadi families in Bombay. Their clan and the Moses family were so attached to each other that Abie, Molly's brother, married Elizabeth (Liza), Alfy's sister. That marriage, too, has flourished.

Liza and "her man"

You can't say you've eaten in Sydney until you sit at the abundant table of Alfy and Molly. Molly makes all the Baghdadi dishes that we grew up with in Bombay and her cooking takes you back, nostalgically, to childhood meals in our hometown. The tastes of her *halbah*, *kooba*, *bamya* and curries are a continued enticement to return. Molly also makes terrific *aloomakala* and has updated her recipe to improve its cholesterol statistics.

The hospitality of my Moses cousins doesn't end there. On one of my visits to Sydney, Liza and I headed for the fish market. She led me straight to a particularly overstocked corner of the market and told me, "Now, you will meet My Man." (Wait a second, where was Abie?) Of course, she meant her fishmonger, who, she swears, gets her the best catch in the market. Together they picked out three huge barramunda, which he cleaned and cut them up for us to take home. I realized that we were in for some very serious cooking.

Crabs bite and Jewfish

Back home Liza asked Abie if he could help her in the kitchen. He was busy, he said, and had not signed on for a day of cooking. "Yes, yes, I know," Liza assured him, "but just see what we're doing here. Just for a few minutes. Please." Just like the barramunda Abie knew he'd been hooked.

Abie loves to cook as much as Liza and they work together in their kitchen like dancing partners. He has a handsome grill on the balcony outside their dining area where he does the frying so that the house doesn't smell. Abie fried the onions first. Then he laid them on paper towels on cookie trays. Then, to my surprise, he took the used oil and poured it under some bushes. 'Wasn't he in danger of killing them?' I asked. Abie looked at his verdant garden and then at me. "What do you think? Are they dying? I've been doing this for years, and look how everything has grown." No question about it, the trees and plants in Abie's garden are spectacular. So much for a closed mind. Abie was teaching me not only how to fry foods but also how to recycle burnt oils and create beauty.

Liza's kitchen

"Frying is an art," Abie told me on the balcony. "You never use the same oil for more than one food. I change the oil every time I fry an item. This way you can keep the temperature constant and avoid a burnt oil smell in your food. And you must turn the food and not allow the oil to penetrate too deeply so that nothing gets overdone." And so he did. He carefully turned the frying food and not only changed the oil in the pan after each frying but cleaned the pan thoroughly.

Abie frying eggplant

Magnificent Sydney Bay, which flows eastward to the South Pacific, can be seen from both Alfy and Lizas' homes. If you travel due southeast you come to the two islands of New Zealand. At the southernmost tip of the North Island is Wellington, the home of yet another of my Moses cousins, the cousin with a joke and a smile, Korda. Aslan Moses, whom we all miss, said of his brother, "Korda is the happiest of all of us." And he knew because they had always been joined at the hip.

Aslan and Korda on Derby Street, Sydney

Korda is the only member of the Moses family who has become
a Kiwi. He is married to a native born New Zealander, Elizabeth
Greer, whose family traces back to Sir Francis Drake, the gallivanting
explorer. Korda and I talk about our days in Bombay. Many of the boys
in Byculla, he told me, were unable to play on Maccabi sports teams,
even though they were good athletes, because they didn't have the 12
annas monthly membership fee. "We didn't even have the money for
the tram or bus fare from Byculla to Fort. People in the Fort area didn't
understand." Still, Korda learned to play backgammon well enough to
go on to win championships in New Zealand. According to Liz he has
been ranked the top backgammon player in New Zealand five times.

Somewhere along the way Korda also learned to be a chef. When
I first questioned him about his favorite foods he responded with "I
don't know anything about cooking." But stay at Liz and Korda's and
you will soon find him creating one of his delicious meals, though "no
one," he says, "is allowed in my kitchen when I cook." He has learned
to use Indian spices in a delicate way, and his chicken, followed by
marvelous syllabub with fresh nectarines, makes a perfect meal.

Liz has some fascinating stories to tell about her family. Her paternal Great-great grandmother, Emily Barrow, had a sister named Sarah Ann, who, in 1840, was the first British woman to set foot in Wellington. Her ship was named the Aurora and on arrival Sarah Ann was carried to shore by a sailor named George Mexted. Although he returned to England he retraced his steps to marry the lady he had carried to shore. A Henri de Mexted has been identified as coming to England with William the Conqueror in 1066. The family has laid claim to this historical connection.

Aslan and his sons

Others of Liz's father's line, the Griersons, were part of the MacGregor clan. They were known as "the children of the mist" as continual oppression had driven them into the shelter of the misty Scottish mountains. The name Grierson became Greer when the family moved to Ireland.

The romantic strain of her forefathers was heard during World War II when Jean Greer, Liz's mother, played the love songs of the 1940s for the GIs stationed in Australia. Jean has great skills and not just at the piano. Her garden is a bounty of roses and the aromas from her kitchen are irresistible. Liz shared her mum's recipe for potato salad (pg. 147), which is served for Christmas dinner, summertime in New Zealand.

☙ *Auntie Rosie's Aloomakala*

INGREDIENTS:
2 per person, at least, whole potatoes
turmeric, sprinkle and rub on on potatoes to a light yellow
salt and pepper to taste
corn or olive oil

METHOD:
Peel, salt, pierce and dry the potatoes for 1 hour to allow as much liquid as possible to evaporate.

Rub the potatoes with turmeric and pepper.

In a deep pan, fry potatoes in the oil on medium heat until well browned on all sides.

The potatoes should be crisp and most of the inside flesh will dissolve in cooking. We always ate *aloomakala* with a relish, *halbah*, and Molly's is one of the best (pg. 144).

ೞ *Molly's Aloomakala*

This is a great recipe for the weary: beating up potatoes on the kitchen counter has got to be good for your well being. It's a blast watching Molly beat away. Goes well with roast chicken and Molly's *halbah*.

INGREDIENTS:
2 per person potatoes
turmeric, salt and pepper to taste

METHOD:
Preheat oven to 350 F (175 C)

Parboil peeled potatoes and drain; cut into quarters if large. Sprinkle with spices and put into a brown paper bag. Pound the bag against the kitchen counter.

Remove potatoes from the bag including any small pieces which become crusty; place on a baking pan and bake for 1/2 hour (or more, if you like them crisp).

∞ *Molly's Halbah*

A relish great with *aloomakala, samosas,* curries and *hameem.*

INGREDIENTS:
1 large Tbsp. fenugreek, ground and soaked in boiling water for 4 hours
1 bunch fresh coriander, stems removed
1 cup fresh parsley
2 cloves garlic
1 or 2 green chilies to taste
Juice of 1/2 lemon

METHOD:
Mix all ingredients in a blender to a thick sauce. Add salt while blending; adjust lemon juice & garlic to your taste.

ᑫ *Korda's Chicken in a Crock Pot*

INGREDIENTS:
one large chicken
Spices: turmeric; salt; pepper; mashed garlic; 1 Tbsp. vindaloo paste (available in jars at most Indian markets), or use spices for vindaloo curry (pg. 66)
6 potatoes, peeled and parboiled
10 small carrots, peeled and parboiled

METHOD:
Pierce chicken in several places and rub all spices and paste over it. Put chicken into pot; Cook for 6 hours at 250°F (120°C).

Add par boiled carrots and potatoes to crock for the last half hour.

With a salad this should serve 4 people. Korda freezes leftover stock for future curries.

☙ *Fish Pilau*

Try some green mango chutney with this meal or something spicier if you are so inclined. This is a labor intensive recipe and can be prepped a couple of hours before your meal. While you and your family and friends visit, the fish pilau increases the appetite with its spicy aroma. Serves 10-12.

INGREDIENTS:
1-1/2 cups (340 gm) rice (usually basmati)
1 fresh dill flower, cut up very fine
1 5-6 lb. fish (halibut or cod) cut into 3" square and 1" thick pieces
8 large peeled and sliced potatoes
4 large red onions peeled and sliced
6 large tomatoes cut into large round slices
salt & pepper to taste
1 Tbsp. turmeric

METHOD:
When I visited, Liza began by boiling 4 cups of lightly salted water. She added all the cut-up dill and rice to the water and cooked the rice 3/4 of the way, until most of the water had been absorbed but the rice was still wet. She put the rice into a colander to drain and then attended to the fish. After cutting the fish into pieces, she washed and salted the fish and put it aside for a half hour. She then preheated the oven to 350F.

Meanwhile, Abie was frying the potatoes and dried them on paper towels. He then fried the sliced onions in fresh oil and dried them on paper towels.
Next, Liza placed the sliced fried potatoes in a large covered pot on the stove. She washed the fish thoroughly and, wearing plastic gloves, rubbed it with the turmeric and pepper.

Abie took over and fried the fish pieces and dried them on paper towels. The large pot now had a layer of fried potatoes at the bottom. The next layer was the fried onions. Then a layer of the large slices of fresh tomatoes covered by a layer of half of the drained rice. The fried fish covers the rice and finally is topped with the balance of the drained rice. The pot cooks in the preheated oven for 1 hour.

∝ *Jean's Potato Salad*

INGREDIENTS:
9 medium potatoes
2 medium red onions
olive oil, mayonnaise, lemon juice, salt and black pepper to taste

METHOD:
Boil the potatoes until cooked and still firm; drain and cool in a colander, then peel and cut into bite size pieces; chop the red onions fine.

In a serving plate, coat the potatoes and onions with oil, mayonnaise, lemon juice, salt and pepper; garnish with parsley.

☙ *Syllabub*

(pronounced Ci.li.bub). This recipe was given to Liz by a friend from Yugoslavia. It is a perfect complement to any spicy dish. Be prepared for many calls for seconds.

INGREDIENTS:
6 firm nectarines
1/2 pint (240 ml) whipping cream
grated lemon rind of one lemon
juice of 3/4 lemon
1 Tbsp. white wine
2 Tbsp. sweet butter
1 Tbsp. brown sugar
small jar passion fruit or mango pulp

METHOD:
Halve the nectarines and remove pits; put fruit into shallow baking dish. Melt butter; pour over each half nectarine. Sprinkle with sugar to caramelize. Put into preheated oven at 200°F (95°C) for approx. 10 minutes

Prepare Syllabub Cream as follows:
    Whip cream until soft – do NOT whip to forming of peaks of cream
    Add grated lemon rind and juice to taste
    Add 1 tablespoon dry white wine
    Whip again until light and fluffy like a good face cream

Swirl one teaspoon of pulp on each serving dish. Place two halves of fruit on pulp. Top with cream; swirl a bit more pulp on top of each half.

Isaac and Susanna Sofaer

Susanna Sofaer was born in Hong Kong. Her hard-working parents, Tak-Hoi Chuk and Yau-kook Wong, were both originally from the province of Chekiang in China and in the 1950s they emigrated to Hong Kong to find work in order to feed their large family. Susanna has a deep appreciation and respect for her parents' sacrifices and their model of dedication to family.

Although Susanna and her husband, Isaac, both grew up in large families in Asia, their home lives were quite different. Isaac lived with his parents and grandparents and other family members and was never short of anything even though his life was not luxurious. He was the second son and as such was probably spoilt and indulged and required to work hard only at his studies. Enamoured of culture and music, he is quite a fine pianist. I have fond memories of Isaac at the baby grand in a small nightclub in Double Bay, a Sydney suburb, the two of us singing our hearts out to a jazz classic. His love for music probably led him to the dance contest in Hong Kong where he met Susanna.

Isaac and Susanna were participating in the "Dance for a Million" benefit which raises money for the Hong Kong Community Chest. Contestants dance for hours with only brief breaks; their sponsors contribute to the benefit for every hour they keep at it. Susanna was 23 and working as a secretary and Isaac worked as a chartered accountant in the stock market. They had come to dance with their own partners but Susanna noticed Isaac copying her steps. After 32 hours of nonstop dancing, the event was moved to the TV studio that had sponsored the event. At that point Isaac left with his date. He came back, though, with a friend, Charles Fearn and tried, without success, to speak to Susanna during one of her breaks. A year later they returned to "Dance for a Million" together and danced for 45 hours. Charles was eventually the best man at their wedding.

Isaac and Susanna met dancing

A few weeks after the benefit, Susanna's mother, who did not speak English, kept getting calls for Susanna from what she called "a foreigner." Susanna told her mom to tell the caller to contact her after 5pm. It was Isaac and he had called earlier as he thought Susanna was a schoolgirl and would be home. He had talked the organizer into giving him her phone number. They started to go out and wanted to marry but Isaac's mother did not approve. Isaac left Hong Kong for a year and when he returned they began to see one another again. Twelve years after their first meeting, they tied the knot in a civil ceremony in Hong Kong. Susanna studied Judaism with a rabbi and was eventually converted by Chabad in Brooklyn. She is a dedicated Jew and loves her place in her community of choice.

While I visited Sydney, Susanna offered to share some of her family recipes with me. One morning she asked if I liked chilies. My response was, "oh yes!" She pointed to her back garden where two chili plants were growing. She hadn't planted them, she said. They had simply appeared. A tip she gave me was to add a few chopped small red chilies to a bottle of soy sauce with 1 teaspoon of sugar. Chili Soy Sauce can be used for many dishes.

The chili tree just showed up

Susanna also took me to the fish market but "her man" was in the Chinese section of the market. They picked out a *swimming fish*, as fresh as possible, that the fishmonger killed in front of us. Together with the whole petrale she also bought a salmon filet and I was delighted with the delicious results.

Susanna's Steamed Fish

Isaac is the son of Rachel Kelly and my father's brother Sonny. Auntie Rae was famous as one of the best cooks in Calcutta and Susanna has been diligent in learning even the most tedious of recipes from her. Rachel and Sonny met and married and had three sons and two daughters. He had a subtle humor. When my parents and I went to visit Uncle Aaron, another of my father's brothers, in the 1980s after an absence of many years, Uncle Sonny met us at the door and declared, with a straight face, "Now, there has been great contagion in this house, so no one get too close to each other." Dad and Aaron stopped in their tracks before bursting out crying and hugging each other. We all laughed, quite impressed with Sonny's bit of chicanery.

Now Sonny and Rachel's children are in three continents. Fleur and Myrtle are in Toronto, Sammy and Ellis are in London, and Isaac lives between Sydney and Hong Kong. Fleur and I discussed her mother's great cooking and she shared a favorite recipe that she has improvised into a delicious vegetarian meal. It's called *kutta*, which in Hindi means sour.

ೞ *Congee*

Very much like *shorbah* but cooked with fresh fish. Serves 4-6

INGREDIENTS:
1 cup (227 gm) jasmine rice
2-1/2 cups water
1 - 2 lbs. (450 – 900 gm) salmon filet
salt to taste
any vegetables you want to use that can be steamed.

METHOD:
Put rice and water and salt to taste in a medium size pot; cook and when it comes to a boil reduce the heat. Keep stirring and leave the top ajar. Cook for approximately 3/4 hour until rice is of a soft and sticky consistency.
Add pieces of salmon on top of the rice and steam covered for 5-6 minutes. Remove fish and place on serving dish. Add pea pods, or fresh spinach, or other fast-poaching vegetables; cover and steam for 2-3 min. Turn off heat under the rice and serve veg and rice with salmon.

For additional flavor, you can sprinkle fish with Chili Soy Sauce (pg. 150-151).

Cooking Tip: You can use less or more water depending on how thick you want the congee.

❀ *Steamed Fish*

Susanna says, "If you can't find *swimming fish*, use fish as fresh as possible." Serves 2-3.

INGREDIENTS:
1 fresh whole fish (at least 2 lbs or 908 gm)
2 Tbsp. oil
1 Tbsp. soy sauce (either plain or chili sauce), sprinkled w/raw brown sugar
1 piece of ginger cut in lengths of 2 inches (5 cm)
3 chopped scallions (spring onions) for garnish

METHOD:
Use a large Chinese wok constructed of 5 layers of metal on the base with a stand large enough to hold a platter on the inside of the wok (wok and stand can be purchased in a Chinese market). Boil water in the wok 2 inches deep. Sprinkle ginger over whole fish and place on a serving plate. Salt to taste.

Once water has fully boiled put the plate and fish on the stand in the wok; cover and steam for 10 minutes. (Adjust according to the weight of the fish.) Lift fish plate and put aside. Clean out wok; put back on a low fire; put oil into wok and heat. On the side put a pinch of sugar on a plate and pour soy sauce on it. Sprinkle scallions on top of the fish and when the oil in the wok is hot, pour the hot oil and the soy sauce mixture over the fish.

Serve with steamed rice and stir-fried vegetables on the side.

Cooking Tip: Do not overcook the fish or it will be tough.

∽ *Beetroot Kutta*

Serve with cooked rice. Serves 2 people.

INGREDIENTS:
3 medium beets cut into thin slices and parboiled
1 medium chopped yellow onion fried in olive oil with salt & 2 garlic cloves
1 packet of cubed tofu cooked on medium heat for 5-6 minutes
3 Tbsp. cranberry juice

METHOD:
Add beets and juice to fried onions and garlic and cook for 10 minutes. Add tofu to mixture and cook for 10 minutes.

Israel

Part IV

ଓ *Jonah Brothers*

My first whispered prayer at the Western Wall in Jerusalem was on the afternoon of Erev Rosh Hashanah (Eve of the New Year) 1969. The *Kotel*, as the wall is known, and closed to Israelis for over 20 years, waited expectantly for all to come. And they came. The rabbi, the layman, the *tzadik* (righteous man), the sinner, the parent and the child, the man and the woman, all approached the wall in egalitarian harmony. There was no separation between the men and women during that victorious time. Some prayed, some whispered, some sang *Yerushalayim Shel Zahav* (Jerusalem of Gold), and some cried, especially the many soldiers there, who, after two years, were still giving thanks for the end of the Six-Day War, or mourning the loss of comrades and friends.

Jerusalem of gold

I climbed the enormous stone steps up to the Dome of the Rock, the mosque behind the *Kotel*. As I sat on the stone staircase, the chants of Jewish prayer rose, the bells of the Holy Sepulchre began to chime, and the *muezzim* on the minaret began to chant, calling worshipers to prayer. I remember the unexpected tears of joy and sadness flowing down my face. "Why can't it always be like this ?" Each sound of awe in unison and in peace.

There was now an open road from Egypt through Israel to Jordan and I saw a line of Mercedes Benz making their way from Gaza, undoubtedly full of families eager to visit their relatives in Jordan. We met three Palestinian women in their long black *abayas* when we visited a date oasis near Gaza. They appeared suddenly out of the dunes of the desert and we began an easy conversation with the oldest of them. She said that the two younger women were her daughters-in-law and that her sons were both becoming doctors in Germany. She might have been a Jewish mother bragging of her son, the doctor. After our pleasant visit the three women set out, back into the desert, and disappeared as mysteriously as they had appeared.

My next visit to the *Kotel* was 35 years later on December 2, 2004. I began the day at the bar mitzvah of Ran Mansoor, my cousin Lulu's grandson. Lulu was in high spirits, in and out of conversations with family members throughout the proceeding. A long low wall at right angles to the *Kotel* now exists between men and women, giving both adequate space for prayer but keeping the sexes apart. The place was packed not only with bar mitzvahs but also with the religious in their black garments and wide-brimmed black hats, who came with heart and soul in their prayers and deep involvement with the Torah. A sense of bedlam seems to exist at the wall, but if you know the protocol of Jewish prayer, you can appreciate the depth of feeling and obvious involvement of most of the people there. The crowds made it difficult to reach the wall itself to deposit a scrap of paper, scrawled with a wish, a prayer, a hope for joy, for health, into one of the over laden crevices between the giant stones.

The skin colors and costumes of those at hand represented many of the tribes among the Jewish people: Russians, Kurds, Americans, Ethiopians, Moroccans, Iraqis, French, South African, South American, British, Yugoslav, Bene Israel. The Arabic ululation spilled from adoring women as each son performed his task of reading from the Torah, and was pelted with sweets to symbolize his acceptance into the community.

(Left) Lulu, Pearl and family members watch from above the men's section.
(Right) Avi Mansoor and his Bar Mitzvah son, Ran.

While the "normal" bar mitzvahs of Sephardim and Ashkenazim were taking place, the walkway to the wall was suddenly full of drumbeats. A group from Ethiopia in bold African clothing came dancing and singing. The men and women clapped and laughed and chanted songs of joy and hope from the *Torah*. They carried themselves with dignity and I could only imagine how important it was for them to have come to the *Kotel* all the way from Ethiopia. They were home, at last, after many centuries.

Within minutes, they were followed by a group of women in flowing, brightly dyed saris, who swept onto the scene preceded by large hand-forged brass drums from South India. These were Indian Jews from Cochin, and the drumming took me back to my teens in Bombay when my Jewish friends and I danced on the terrace above an Indian temple. I wanted to join their passionate dance, but my well-schooled sense of decorum stilled my feet.

Last, and most extravagant, came a family group dressed in heavy, bright green, blue, violet, and crimson velvet capes decorated with thick gold threaded designs. A young boy was in a royal blue velvet cape, a gold encrusted cap on his head. He held his arms open to all, with adults who carried him on a chair above the crowd, as if he were young King David returning to his palace. There were flute players and drummers, followed by the boy's entire class from school, together with relatives also dressed in rich velvet robes flowing to the ground. The music was upbeat and the people, of Georgian descent from one of the recently freed states of old Russia, created a tableau of a grand ball in czarist Russia.

My Israeli friends and family said that what we had seen that day was astonishing, and it made me realize that the totality of the Jewish people in Israel represented many peoples of the United Nations. On future journeys, I have put aside time for quiet prayer at the wall for dear ones who are no longer with us; my dearest cousins Aslan and Lulu, my sweet friend Rocky, my father; prayers for my children and grandchildren, and for my life. There is still a lot of prayer in the secular me as well as a lot of the Jewess.

I imagine the sounds of the Roman chariots as I stand on the Cardo.
(Roman Road) Old City, Jerusalem

The golden light of Jerusalem also dances on the terrace flat of my cousins, Alice and Effry Jonah. The sun warms their home from beyond the Judean hills, and visiting them I found myself immersed in the love I felt for the city. Effry was born in Calcutta, Alice in Czechoslovakia. Never a negative word about anyone or anything escapes their lips, and the care they feel for each other extends to every member of their families, and to all their associates and friends. Alice shared a story about how one night early in their marriage, she awoke from a dream and slapped Effry. "I was shocked." Alice explained that in the dream he had been unfaithful to her. She wanted Effry to understand that she would never accept that kind of behavior. Point made; point taken. No hard feelings.

Mum and us – Effry, Rachel and Edmund

Effry and his brother Edmund are the sons of my dad's sister Rachel and her husband, Sass Jonah. I remember Aunt Rachel as the most beautiful, effervescent woman of the Sofaer family. Between the ages of 16 and 18 she starred in a number of Indian films, helping her family financially in Calcutta after they endured heavy business losses in Rangoon. Effry said, "The Jonah and Sofaer families met after the Sofaers left Burma for India. Rachel was 12 and Sass was 21 but he knew then she was the girl he would marry and she soon determined she would marry no other man. Nine years later they married."

Rachel Jonah

During WWII Rachel worked as a Colonel's secretary at the American army base. She organized dances at the Agarpara Club of the B. N. Elias jute mill, where Effrys' father was an executive. A very active person, she helped several of the GIs wives keep abreast of their husbands and sent them gift packages. In the Tiger Rag, the newspaper for American G.I.s in India, she was referred to in a headline as an "Angel in Our Midst."

Aunt Rachel died in childbirth with her baby in April 1948, just three months after her sister Iris died giving birth to her namesake, my cousin Iris, now living in India. Effry was only 14 and Edmund 12. Grandpa Meyer Sofaer had always been a deeply religious man, but the shock of losing two daughters within three months was too hard for him to bear and he stopped his daily prayers after that. He told me one day, "There is no God if he can be so cruel. I don't believe in him anymore." From that time on, he became very bitter and silent.

Effry and Edmund grew up in a suburb of Calcutta, Agarpara, where, for three months every year, they had a full and indulged life. They spent the rest of the year at boarding school in Mt. Abu, Rajputana, which was about 2,000 miles from Calcutta and the potential approach of the Japanese army. After the war, they completed their studies at St. Joseph's College, Darjeeling, in the Himalayan Mountains, closer to home.

With all their luxury they were still very uncomfortable during the hot weather. There was no private air-conditioning in those days and all they could do was to sit under the *punkas* (fans). As Uncle Sass had 4,000 to 5,000 people working under him, he could seldom leave the factory and holiday in the cooler hill stations like other families did. Effry says, "Whenever my parents went to Calcutta they'd go to the cinema where there was air-conditioning. It didn't matter what movie was playing, they'd go to the air-conditioned cinema." Edmund recalls that once a year, during the Pujah holidays, when all factories and schools shut down, his parents would leave the heat of the plains and come up to Darjeeling for 10 days and take the boys out of school to stay with them in their hotel.

Effry met Alice in Canada. After studying in England to be an accountant, he had moved to Canada in 1959. A counselor at the Jewish Community Center introduced him to Alice and they married in September 1962. Alice's father, Hans Lederer, had moved to Canada with his family in 1939 and was able to obtain resident papers because he had 16 years of farming experience in Israel. Both Alice and Effry were inspired by their Judaism and after several journeys to Israel, they made *Aliyah* (immigration or return to the Land of Israel) in August 1979. Their children, who were

Canadian born, had attended a Hebrew day school and were so taken with Israel that the move seemed natural.

Alice resting after Hanukah dinner

Alice had fallen in love with Israel as a girl listening to her father's stories of his kibbutz he had helped to start in 1923 as a young Zionist. Alice said he wept when the United Nations voted for the right of a state of Israel. She had been immersed, from her childhood, with reminisces of family members who had been caught up in the storm of World War II, unable to experience the freedom her father felt in Israel. For her, Israel was home. And when she saw her first sunset in Jerusalem, the vision touched her to her core. Her children have the same devotion and passion to their small country.

Hospitality and love are showered upon all visitors to Alice and Effry's home The kitchen usually has five or six dishes being prepared at the same time, while the oven bakes delectable pastries from Alice's

Czech heritage. To say she is a great cook is an understatement. Her long and somewhat warped table groans with the weight of the delicious foods. On one occasion, a guest said, "If you put another dish on the table it will break." Alice put another dish down and the table broke. The reaction of one and all was to pick up the food, adjust the table and enjoy dinner while Ruth and JJ, two of Alice and Effrys' children, jumped under the table and continued the puzzle that had fallen off. Alice willingly shared recipes I had the pleasure to enjoy at their table. She has learned how to cook our traditional Baghdadi/Indian foods from her father-in-law, Sass Jonah, and has now surpassed most of us. She had to learn, as Effry adores the food he grew up with in India and has special memories of Nachums, the bakery that made all the *machboos* for the Jewish people in Calcutta, like Sameha did in Bombay.

It is amazing that Alice has the time to make as many dishes as she does every week. She is the cultural director of a shelter for elderly former citizens of the Soviet Union. They now have a choir under Alice's tutelage and she has organized outings and other activities for them. She gets a very small salary, most of which she uses to help pay for the residents' doctors bills and other needs.

On my recent trip to Jerusalem, I noticed the members of the Jonah family telephoned one another every day. "Where will you be today?" "I'm going to be at such and such market, can I pick up something for you?" Or, "Do you need a ride?" I was impressed by the connection within the family and their willingness to help each other. I also realized that they each, especially Effry, wanted to know the location of everyone during the day in case there was a bombing.

Jerusalem is a city of the "Abrahamic" religions. They come from the same source. If only they could respect one another and be in peace. In the Old Testament even David had to run away to the desert garden of Ein Gedi from the fury of King Saul. People of many faiths have hidden from war in the mountain caves above the Sea of Galilee. David hid in the caves of the Ein Gedi waterfalls among the ibex, snakes and leopards of that time. Ein Gedi is barren and verdant; secrets are encrusted in the patina of massive rocks; tranquility plays her flute in the pools of waterfalls; the echoes of silence enter my soul. To me, Ein Gedi is the most peaceful place in Israel.

David's Wadi – Ein Gedi

Jordan and an ibex in the Ein Gedi Reserve

Jordan is directly across the healing waters of the Galilee. The ibex have been nurtured back from near extinction and they roam the

Ein Gedi Reserve in large families. Above them the eagles once again roam the desert highlands. History of the ages surrounds the visitor as in most parts of Israel. Perhaps this will be the place where the lion and the deer lie down together in peace.

Edmund – man with a camera

Edmund, like his older brother, Effry, was born in Calcutta. He seems to have been born with the thespian genes of the Sofaers as he has always been very interested in music, theater, the arts and writing (he has written a book). Edmund recalls having a very difficult time coping with the loss of his mother and the absence of his brother when Effry went to England for his education. He says he never felt "at ease" in India after the death of his mother. He worked successfully in the tobacco business with B. N. Elias in Andra Pradesh for four years, but his heart wasn't in it. Finally he left India in May 1958 to join Effry to London. When he told his Dad that he wished to be an actor, the response he got was "Do what you damn well like."

The Six-Day War of 1967: "I was so moved and concerned during the fighting that I made my way to Israel, leaving my pregnant wife in London. I arrived shortly after the war in June and realized that my heart and soul belonged to Israel." He and Molly and their infant daughter, Sharone, moved to Tel Aviv in 1968 and their two sons, Maurice and Yuval, were born there.

In Tel Aviv, Edmund was one of the founding members of the English Theater and the Shakespeare Reading Circle. These were only the start of many steps into the theater but, as he had to support his family, it was an avocation instead of a full-time job. Although his mother had been an actress in her teens in Calcutta, the family never took the acting field seriously. If only they would have given Edmund a chance. After hearing him quote Shakespeare non-stop, I am sure he would have been in step with Abraham Sofaer, doyen of the British stage and later a Hollywood actor. He would have had a lot more fun in his life and perhaps been a great success. In addition to his knowledge of the theater, he is well versed in cinema and music. He knows who acted in, produced and directed films; he can tell you the composers and the lyrics of Big Band music; he is a walking jazz encyclopedia.

And, a whiz in the kitchen. He cooked a delicious *bamya kutta* with *koobas* and other delicacies for lunch. The table was already set when we arrived and he hovered in the kitchen as if he were directing the first act of a play. We were lucky to be the players in the second act on his stage as we scraped our plates with satisfaction. What a guy! I have raved about him to other Sofaer cousins around the world and of course they all want to meet him. Here are some of Edmund's and Alice's star recipes.

ℭ *Alice's Marag*

Serve with boiled white rice and *halbah*. Serves 10

INGREDIENTS:
1 large onion, cut up
1 Tbsp. Oil
1 tsp. Ground ginger
1 tsp. Ground garlic plus 2 cloves
1 chicken skinned and cut in pieces, plus 2 legs and 2 thighs (Effry prefers dark meat).
2 medium potatoes, cut up
3 medium tomatoes parboiled, peeled and mashed
6 cups water
salt and pepper to taste
1 cup freshly cut-up coriander

METHOD:
Saute onion in oil with garlic and ginger. Add the chicken with half a cup of water. Cook slowly on low flame for about ten minutes. While this is cooking, boil the rest of the water and add it (after the 10 minutes) together with the potatoes, salt & pepper and the tomatoes.

Cook on medium heat until chicken is done (approximately 45 min.)

Add coriander. (Optional: add 1 cup parboiled chick peas)

☙ *Alice's Halbah*

Hot relish to use with *shoofta*, etc. and save in refrigerator.

INGREDIENTS:
8 tsp. fenugreek seeds, soaked a few hours, boiled for 1/2 hour and drained,
or
8 tsp. powdered fenugreek.
2 cups lemon juice
fresh green chili to taste
3 cloves garlic
2 tsp. ginger
1 tsp. turmeric
salt to taste
Up to 2 small bunches of fresh cilantro, cut up and cleaned with no stems
Optional: add small amount of fresh mint or parsley

METHOD:
Blend together.

◌ *Schnitzel*

Serves 6-8.

INGREDIENTS:
10 pieces of chicken or turkey
1 egg
1 small onion
2 Tbsp. white vinegar,
1 Tbsp. ketchup
1 tsp. mustard powder
2 cloves garlic
1 tsp. ginger
1 tsp. turmeric
1 tsp. salt
matzo meal or bread crumbs or a combination of both

METHOD:
Remove any fat from meat and pound with meat hammer to make more tender.

Make a marinade by mixing the rest of the ingredients (except matzo meal) in a food processor. Marinate the meat for as long as possible, preferably overnight.

Cover each piece with matzo meal or bread crumbs. Fry on medium heat in a minimum amount of cooking oil and drain on a paper towel.

∞ *Kooba Soup*

Serves 8-10.

INGREDIENTS:
1 chopped medium onion
1 turnip, cubed
1 parsnip, cubed
1 carrot, sliced
1 zucchini, cubed
1 stalk celery
2 leaves of chard
1/2 cup mashed pumpkin
6 stalks of cilantro, no stems, chopped
salt and pepper to taste
dash Tabasco sauce
5 cups water

METHOD:
In a stock pot, fry onion in a little oil. When light brown add the vegetables, salt and pepper and Tabasco sauce, then saute until brown. Add boiling water. The Koobas should be added later and heated with the soup before serving.

 **Koobas**

for Kooba Soup

INGREDIENTS:
2 skinless, boneless chicken breasts, finely chopped
1 small chopped onion
1/2 cup chopped cilantro, no stems
dash salt
1 cup semolina
1 cup rice powder
1/3 tsp. salt
1 cup approx. water
1/2 cup approx. vegetable oil

METHOD:
Mix chicken with onion, cilantro and dash of salt.

Make a paste of semolina, rice powder and salt sprinkled with just enough water and oil to achieve the consistency of a pliable pastry dough. Cover the dough, removing a small amount at a time while making the koobas. Smooth a small piece of dough and cup in the palm of your hand. Place meat mixture inside and close dough around the meat to form into a ball. Cover balls with cloth until ready to cook. Do this until the mixtures are used up. Drop balls into boiling water and boil gently until balls float up. Remove with slotted spoon and add to the soup.

☜ *Chocolate Mousse Pie*

This is a kosher dessert

INGREDIENTS:
6 oz (180 gm) good semi-sweet chocolate (without milk)
3/4 cup (200 gm) margarine
6 eggs, separated
2 cups (454 gm) sugar
Few grains instant coffee
1/4 cup (60 ml) brandy or non-milk liqueur
5 Tbsp. flour
1/2 tsp. baking powder

METHOD:
Melt the chocolate with the margarine and put aside. Beat the egg whites with the sugar and remove from the mixer. Beat the yolks, add the brandy and coffee and stir into the chocolate mix. Fold into the egg whites. Remove 1/3 and fold into flour and baking powder. Spread onto lightly greased container (a glass or earthenware quiche form is good). Bake at 350°F (175°C)for 15 minutes.

When cool add the remaining chocolate mixture. Place in freezer to set. Topping if desired: swirl chocolate syrup on the cake. Freeze again.

Remove from freezer 20 minutes before serving

❦ *Dolmas*

Makes a zesty and easy hors d'oeuvre. Stuffed grape leaves can be purchased in Middle East stores

Place 1 bottle of ready made dolmas on baking pan. Mix a little chopped ginger and garlic and the best thick honey with a drop of sweet vinegar (not the malt type - the light one) and pour over the dolmas. Cover lightly with tin foil and set aside for 1-2 hours.

Bake in a preheated 325° F (165°C) oven for 10-15 minutes, until the stuffing has absorbed the paste flavor.

ℭℨ *Uncle Sass and Family*

My father's younger brother Sassoon was born in 1919 in Rangoon, Burma, which was then a part of the British Empire. He was just nine years old when he and his family moved to Calcutta. Sass recalls with great fondness his school days in Calcutta at St. Xavier's and his favorite teacher, Father Weaver. He and my father were both involved in theater and Sass was able to quote much of Shakespeare by heart. The great Indian poet Rabindranath Tagore visited the school's drama department, and, according to Sass, he shook hands with the student actors and complimented them on their performance.

Sass and my father usually played cricket together. One day my father accidentally hit Sass in the eye with the ball. "Can you believe it," Sass says, "nothing happened to my eye." And indeed, they would never have hurt each other. To me, they are very much alike in their grace and intelligence. David would worry when Sass got dirty after playing outside. Their father would lose his temper and beat the boys if any of them came home dirty. Now how does an active boy stay clean playing outside? David would get anxious about the beating and, as Sass tells it, would repeat their father's line, "Cleanliness is not only keeping your body clean, but keeping your stomach clean." Sounds like a confused message to me but whatever worked. My Uncle Sass reminds me of how much I miss my dad.

Sass's future wife, Ruth Galiah, was lovingly nicknamed "Girlie" by her family of three brothers growing up in Ahamdebad, India. Her father came to India from Yemen and her mother from Baghdad. She too was educated at a Catholic school and she was determined to show her teachers that she knew the Bible as well as the non-Jewish girls. "I purposely became so smart with the New Testament that I was able to quote many passages by heart to impress the Nuns," she says. She had a wonderful childhood that was full of music with her brothers Sass and Solly, who eventually had their own band. Girlie played the piano and had a great voice so she was a vital part. Girlie does not play the piano anymore but I can still hear her playing any song you could come up with without a moment's hesitation. I loved singing with her.

Sofaer clan at wedding of Uncle Sass and Aunt Girlie

Sass and Girlie met in Bombay, and when they married, I was one of their flower girls (I seem to have been a flower girl countless times). They lived in Sobani Mansions with their two daughters, Florence (Flo) and Rebecca (Becky), along with Granny and Grandpa, Uncle Sonny and Auntie Rae and their family; Auntie Ramah and Irene lived next door. Flo and Becky, used to living as an extended family, now live that way on a moshav in Shoresh, Israel. Their parents and one of Flo's sons and his family have homes there, too.

Uncle Sass remembers riots between Hindus and Muslims in Calcutta years before partition. His brother Aaron hid some Muslims in their family's warehouse and Uncle Sass enthusiastically wrote a story to share at their school. Aaron quickly stopped him from turning it in. He knew it could create trouble for the Sofaers as some

Hindus were against any help for Muslims. Uncle Sass had to tear up his story.

All my father's brothers worked in the import/export business to some extent. Uncle Sass had his own business, the Burma Stores in Poona, for many years. During the war business was booming as British and American soldiers bought coffee, sugar, chocolates and many other hard-to-get staples to ship to their families back home. I was hired to grind and weigh out coffee, and in spite of my lack of expertise, Uncle Sass taught me patiently and even paid me a few rupees. I felt very grown up. After the war and the departure of the soldiers, the Burma Stores business came to a halt.

Aunt Iris and Uncle Abey in Poona

One summer when I visited Poona as a child, an amazing incident took place in the home of my aunt Iris. She had lost a ring and, after a thorough search of the house, there was no doubt that it had been stolen. A man was brought to the house carrying a large Old Testament and a very large key. He placed the key in chapter 32 of Numbers on line 23, which read, "And be sure your sin will find you out," then closed the book with part of the key sticking out. The adults sat around a table where the book was placed and I was told to be quiet." I became a fly on the wall. The man called out the names, one at a time, of all the people who had been around the house. Nothing happened until one particular name was called, the book turned in a 360 degree circle, and the key fell out of the book. That particular person was found and had, in fact, taken the ring.

For many years I remembered this incident and wondered if I hadn't imagined the whole thing. On a journey to Israel I asked my uncle Sassoon about it. With a look of delight, he told me the identical story. Later I mentioned it to his daughter Flo, and her eyes lit up. She was very surprised and said, "My gram was there and told me the same story." It was a relief to know that what I had remembered had really happened.

Sass and Girlie decided to move to England in late 1952 to start a new life. Effry stayed with them in 1953 when he first went to England for studies, with Edmond and his father, following four years later. The family from Bombay was congregating in London. "The children received an excellent education but life was very hard in London," Auntie Girlie recalls. In 1966 they eventually decided to move to Israel, where they had friends and family and it was warmer. Now the Jonahs and Uncle Sass and his family are all in Israel with many sabra (native-born Israeli) children and grandchildren.

I ate with them in their flat overlooking the magnificent Judean Hills and after dinner noticed a Sofaer DNA aberration that seems to cross oceans. The two of them prepared supper together but after we had eaten Sass said, "I'm washing up Girlie. Don't touch a thing." Where had I heard these words before? My brother Ike insists that only he can stack a dishwasher. He will simply say, "I'm fine," and take over. My father always said to my mother, "Don't touch anything." My brother Abe seems to be the head dishwasher in his household. Is this attachment to washing up by our Sofaer men an incredible trait that women around the world would love to have in their men? Are we sitting on a formula that could keep marriages together?

Uncle Sass was happy to share the recipe for dessert, his homemade fruit sauce. He always has some on hand: "It's good for my body." And discussing the curry, the more onions in the base of an Indian curry, he advises, the tastier and thicker the sauce.

Flo has lived with her friend Warner Kenton in Shoresh for many years. She is active as a counselor and healer, computer whiz and good friend to many members of the moshav. In Israel, where everyone lives for each day, not knowing who will be blown away next, there is a great need for the kind of healing and support she offers.

Kebabs in Jerusalem – Standing from left: Shalom, Pearl, Uncle Sass, Aunt Girlie and Becky. Seated from left: Effry, Stephanie, Ruth and Flo

Warner was born in London. His father came from Russia, his mother from Chile. This connection of two vastly different continents seems to have created one of the world's gentler human beings. Warner is head cook in the kitchen and loves spicy Indian food. He tried to grow a chili tree and, after failing for two years, realized that a tree had grown outside their kitchen window from a chili that had fallen near his digging. He now uses countless chilies ("to taste") in a Parsi dish that he prepares.

Becky is married to Shalom Mevorach, a sabra (native-born Israeli) of Yemenite heritage. Becky is a flourishing artist and teacher.

Their home houses ample studio space and storage for her abundant paintings and sculpture and a huge variety of useful creations. Even the garden boasts some of her elegant stone work.

Warner and his magical chilies

Becky showed me what in Israel is called their "safe room," explaining that every house in the moshav has to have one or you can't get a final permit. In their house, the room is in the basement with a duct for outside air, masks, foods, water and clothing. She is an incredible cook and she gave me some of her special recipes. The Lemon Pickle is not only super simple, it's a great recipe for the abundance of lemons growing in most gardens of California.

Becky's sculpture garden

❧ *Fruit Sauce*

Collect approximately 2 pounds (1 kg) of all kinds of fresh fruit - "the more the merrier," says Uncle Sass. "I use 7-10 varieties." Peel and cut up. Add 1 tsp. clear gelatin. Add grape juice for sweetness. Bring ALL to a boil. Mash and cool, – "nothing more."

ೞ *Chicken Dhansak*

Serve with boiled basmati rice. This can be cooked with fish, vegetables or eggs instead of chicken. Warner uses about 20 small red chilies – for brave hearts, go for it! Have plenty of cold water ready. Serves 4-6.

INGREDIENTS:
1 cup red dahl (mansoor) cooked until soft
5 chopped yellow onions fried in oil
6-10 cutup small red chilies
2 lbs. (1 kg.) partly cooked chicken pieces
4 tomatoes in paste form
1 Tbsp. sugar
1/2 tsp. tamarind
1 tsp. Asafoetida powder (available in Indian grocery stores)
1/2 tsp. ginger
1/2 tsp. curry powder
 cumin, coriander and garlic to taste

METHOD:
Add cooked dahl to fried onions and chilies; add and brown chicken quickly; add all spices and cook 15 minutes; add the tomato paste; cook on low for at least 1/2 hour. Serve with fresh boiled rice.

♋ *Lemon Pickle*

I keep my pickle in the refrigerator and it is ready to spice up many meals fast.

INGREDIENTS:
About 4 lbs. (2 kg) thick-skinned yellow lemons
Approx. I cup (227 gm) fine salt
1/3 cup (100 gm) chili powder OR paprika OR equal mixture of both
1/2 cup (114 gm) olive oil

METHOD:
Slice washed lemons into 1cm thickness. Mix chili/paprika with the salt. Dip lemon slices into spice mixture as if getting ready to fry. Place lemon slices in an airtight jar, layer upon layer. Close the jar for 3 days until juice from the lemons is evident in the jar. Remove lemon juice and pour equal amount of fresh lemon juice over lemon slices; Add the oil to avoid rotting; Close tight – ready in about 10-14 days.

☙ *Becky's Moroccan Fish*

Serve with fresh boiled rice. Serves 4.

INGREDIENTS:
1 bunch chopped cilantro – no stems
1 can (12oz. – 340 grams) chickpeas
1 large carrot sliced thin vertically
lemon pickle
2-3 lbs. (1 - 1.5 kg) fish filets cut thick
5-10 cloves crushed garlic – to taste
1/3 cup olive oil
3-4 tsp. paprika
1 tsp. dried or fresh chopped chilies
salt – to taste
1 cup (240 ml) lemon juice mixed with water

METHOD:
Lay half of cilantro on bottom of pan; cover with chick peas. Cover with carrots; cover with chopped Lemon Pickle; cover with garlic. Lay filets of fish over the pickle and garlic. Mix oil, paprika, chilies and salt; sprinkle mix gently over fish. Sprinkle a little of lemon and water mix over the fish. Sprinkle balance of cilantro on top. Bring all to a boil on a high fire; lower to lowest flame and cover 30-40 minutes. Shake pan to keep fish from burning; sprinkle lemon/water if fish seems dry.

London
and New York

Part V

⊗ *On Stage*

Isaac Sofaer, my grandfather Meyer's brother, inspired a colorful history with his major architectural contributions to the city of Rangoon (Yangon) in Burma. Many of the most beautiful and structurally sound buildings in Rangoon were drafted by Isaac's hand. My father remembered the lake around a holiday house Isaac built named *Jagnamara* ("the sixth mile" out of Rangoon). He created the famous Chong Tsong palace in Rangoon, the headquarters of the Young Communists when we visited in 1984. We were not permitted entrance. Instead, my father and I walked around Rangoon looking for the Sofaer Buildings. He was able to identify them from the entry tiles as he was with Isaac when the tiles were purchased. The truly extraordinary part of this story is that Isaac never studied architecture.

As we walked the streets, Dad remembered an earthquake that had occurred when he was a teenager in Rangoon:

> I was working in Uncle Isaac's bakery at that time, and suddenly the earth shook. I ran to Uncle Isaac's house, which was an old, simple wooden structure, while houses were falling down around me. Uncle Isaac's family were fine and their house stayed standing. Then I ran to Mr. Tobeson, my boss at the bakery, and begged for bread for the many poor people on the streets. Tobeson called me a 'sentimental fool,' but after much cajoling on my part, he gave in and I was soon on a truck distributing over 20,000 pounds of bread, just out of the ovens, with a revolver in my pocket. Tobeson insisted that I carry a gun even though I had no idea what to do with it. When I returned to the bakery I turned to my boss and said, 'Mr. Tobeson, you have enough blessings today to fly you to heaven.'

Uncle Sass confirms that there was an earthquake when he was a boy in Calcutta. He writes, "In 1930, there took place a disastrous earthquake in North Western India, in Dhubri, in the province of Assam. This quake was felt in most parts of central; north western; and south western India, including Burma and elsewhere. Thus I feel sure it must have been part of the Rangoon earthquake of 1930."

Young David Sofaer

Amazingly, Dad was to meet Tobeson again, years later, in Bombay. My parents had heard of a restaurant in Bombay where they served steaks and hamburgers. With our new American tastes, we headed there. The maitre d' greeted my mother and the four of us kids and then Dad walked in. He and Tobeson took one look at each other and fell into each other's arms. We became regulars at Mr. Tobeson's restaurant.

Isaac married Ramah Solomon, also of Baghdad, and had a large family. Their eldest son, Abraham Sofaer, wanted to be an actor from a very young age and was fanciful enough to fall in love with the name "Psyche" when he studied the Greek tragedies. While in his teens, he made the bold statement, "When I marry, I will marry a girl named Psyche."

But I'm getting ahead of the story. In 1920 Abraham was sent to Oxford to study law and Isaac warned him that if he abandoned his studies, he would be cut off financially. Abraham lasted three days at Oxford and moved to London. His father kept his word. Abraham quickly tried out for any part possible in a musical called *The Lilac Domino*. He couldn't dance, he couldn't sing, but he got a part. He was so hopeless that the principal dancer took pity on him, helping him in rehearsals and even teaching him how to apply make-up. And that's how they met. And fell in love. Besides his good looks and charm, he courted her with penny bars of chocolate. Amazingly enough, her name was Psyche. Is this serendipity or an instance of "if you dream it enough, it will be yours." They soon married and eventually had six children.

Very quickly Abraham began to perform with the Old Vic at Stratford-on-Avon. Perhaps it was that wonderful voice and the confident Sofaer presence that soon moved him into roles with top performers like Helen Hayes. Abraham directed *The Merchant of Venice*, playing Shylock to her Portia. This starring combination led them to Broadway, where she played the Queen in *Victoria Regina* with him in the role of Disraeli. The Broadway production was followed by a tour around the United States. Hollywood began to notice. Abraham became a well-known film actor, appearing in many films, among others, *Elephant Walk* with Elizabeth Taylor, *Bhowani Junction* with Ava Gardner, and *Stairway to Heaven* with David Niven.

In reality, Abraham's fame paled in comparison with the theater history of Psyche's family. Her mother was Katie Cohen, daughter of Fanny Harrison, the original Ruth in Gilbert & Sullivan's *Pirates of Penzance* and the first Fairy Queen with D'Oyly Carte's No. 2 *Iolanthe* company. Katie followed her mother performing many Gilbert & Sullivan roles. Albert Christian, Psyche's father, also had many roles with the various D'Oyly Carte companies, and when he and Psyche's mother toured America in 1893 with Lottie Collins, he was billed as "D'Oyly Cartes' leading baritone."

Gilbert & Sullivan was beloved by all the Sofaers who grew up in Rangoon, and they passed their passion on to their children. My first experience of formal theater was a production of *H.M.S. Pinafore* at the Governor's Mansion in Bombay. I went with my dad and we sat in the front row in the garden overlooking the Indian Ocean. Dad quietly sang the songs with the performers and he was delighted with the afternoon. What a lovely way to see a first formal performance.

Psyche grew up living both with her traveling parents and in the Grosvenor House suite of her aunt, Lady Lyons of the famous Lyons Corner Houses in England. Her aunt, who was also named Psyche, indulged her niece. According to my cousin David, Abraham's son, "She more or less raised my mother." As a result, Psyche had a colorful and elaborate life. Lady Lyons would occasionally leave her alone in her late teens, unaware of Psyche's fearless mind and body. During holidays in Brighton, Psyche tried out daring feats on private excursions. She made friends with a man in Brighton who cooperated with her fanciful ideas. The most outrageous was tying Psyche in a sack and dropping her off the pier into the water. Psyche would then get out of the sack and make her way to the beach. She shared her secret with her daughter Ruth: "He would put me in the sack and I would quickly take a large loop of the rope into the sack with me. Then when he knotted the sack, I would let go of the rope, loosening the knot so that I could push the top open and get out." Houdini had nothing on this lady.

The transition from dancing to motherhood kept Psyche on her toes in their London home. In 1936, the children Pat, David and Ruth entered a costume competition in their school. Ruth said, "My mother went to the British Museum and drew copies of Nefertiti's jeweled collar." Psyche made costumes for Ruth and David and rented a costume of Mary, Queen of Scots for Pat; David went as a hot water bottle made out of paper; Ruth was Queen Nefertiti. First, her mother put Ruth into a bath of permanganate of potash to dye her body brown. Then she copied the costume from her drawings at the museum almost to perfection. The children won all the prizes for best costumes, much to the consternation of the rest of the school. And Ruth went back to her whiter complexion with copious rubbings.

David, her brother, had absolutely no idea what it meant to be a Jew. All he knew was that he was English. He remembers a household of constant yelling and screaming with his father, a major domo tyrant, and his mother, the loving and nurturing one. David followed his parents path into the world of entertainment and became a stage manager of theater, opera and dance in London and San Francisco. Eventually he moved to Los Angeles, where he lived near his second love, a sailboat berthed in Marina del Rey. He had a friend there named Tom Ferguson who came to him one day and said, "Who's this guy Abe Sofaer?" "Well, that's my father." "No, no," said Tom. "I met him in Washington and had lunch with him. He's your cousin." Tom had met my brother Abe, who encouraged my father to contact his cousin Abraham. Dad wrote to Abraham and the next time David visited his father he was shown my dad's letter. Abraham was reluctant to get in touch but David urged him to make a connection with his cousin and helped him write an answer. That's how they reconnected for the first time, at the Motion Picture Actors Home in Los Angeles, since they were boys in Rangoon.

Pat still lives in Northern England, Ruth, Judy and Susannah live in Southern California, and their brother, David, lives on Orcas Island. Abraham began to paint after he and he Psyche retired in Santa Barbara. He copied the great masters and his works live happily on the walls of all his children. I was taken aback when I first visited Susannah and saw what looked like original Monets, Manets, Lautrecs and other impressionists adorning every room in the house. Psyche's work, too, based on Native American themes are impressive.

Susannah remembers some of her father's favorite expressions: "*Bitil kalb!*" (child of a dog) and "*Su-war ka bucha!*" (child of a swine) — melodic curses of our Arab and Indian backgrounds, respectively. It took her and her siblings years to realize the potency of these vivid explosions, which both delighted them and caused them fear, as their father used them in anger but with a smile.

Susannah recalls how her sister Judy once found herself in an elevator with Gene Kelly. Judy turned to him and said, "Mr. Kelly, I have danced every one of your dances with you, by myself." At this, Gene Kelly bowed, took Judy's hand, and with the rest of the passengers backed to the walls, Judy and Gene moved smoothly within the space of an elevator.

Susannah and I have talked about our fathers and how neither of them ever cooked but invariably had something to say about the salt. There was never enough salt. Even though she added loads of spices and salt to the *bhagi* (vegetable dish), there was always the critical "not enough salt." Susannah once had the temerity to explain to her father that as people got older their taste buds were not as sensitive. "Oh God! Why is everything my fault?" he retorted. "Needless to say," Susannah remembers, "in all the years I schlepped that bloody *bhaji* down to him he never once said thank you. Amazing. The minute I put it in front of him he dove into it like a starving man and, except to complain, never said another word to me!" At the end of this chapter, you'll find the famous *bhagi*, one of the staples of any Indian diet.

Another of her father's favorite foods was Gangi Chicken. Abraham liked Psyche to cook chicken in a particular way and Psyche eventually became adept at all the foods from Burma and India that her sisters-in-law readily shared with her. When Deborah, Susanna's daughter, was a little girl, she called her granny "Gangi." Hence, the chicken recipe became known as Gangi Chicken.

Ruth Sofaer has inherited the "genes of design" from her grandfather Isaac. As an architectural designer in the Los Angeles area, she has enhanced many famous homes with her keen eye and panache. She recalls that when she worked with builders and gardeners, she often squatted if they were involved with placing pipes in the ground or laying floors. Her father, whom she adored, saw her in such a position once when some men were pouring concrete and he said with a smile, "You do so many things like my father. He would get down on the ground with his men to explain what he wanted."

When they were old, Abraham and Psyche eventually lived at the Motion Picture Actors Home. My parents, David and Mozelle, went to visit them there and the two cousins saw one another for the first time since Sofaer & Company went bankrupt. Abraham was in England at the time and had no idea what had taken place, only that his father, Isaac, did not see his brother Meyer anymore. Dad explained the full story to Abraham, which he had witnessed during the meeting between their fathers after the bankruptcy.

He said that while his father, Meyer, was on one of his trips around the world, an accountant in one of their banks realized that Isaac had overextended their loans. The accountant and bankers spoke to Isaac and asked him to provide some monies against the loans. It seems that Isaac lost his temper. His response was, "Don't you know who I am? How dare you question me about money?" The bankers immediately called in the loans. Meyer was the brother who dealt with finances, and by the time he got back to Rangoon the Sofaer fortune was gone. On Meyer's return, his brother Isaac came to his house crying and blaming himself for their problems. Meyer turned to his brother and said that it was a great shame that such things had taken place in his absence. Then he paused, welcomed his brother to sit down, and offered him some tea. No other words or recriminations were ever made but that was the last time the brothers ever saw each other. Susannah feels that Abraham always carried Isaac's guilt on his shoulders but that after meeting David, and hearing the story about what had happened in Rangoon, her father was much more at peace.

Brothers Meyer Sofaer (front) and Isaac Sofaer (back) in
front of Sofaer building

Even when he was dying Abraham created a great deal of drama around himself. There were many calls of "This is it. Come at once, he's going." But he carried on. There was, inevitably, a final call, and the whole family gathered around him. They heard him say, "Promise me, you must all promise me something." And they all leaned in. "Yes, Daddy." "Promise me you will never vote Republican!" They all collapsed with screams of laughter. Meanwhile the nurses, who were in love with him, were coming in one after the other, crying their eyes out (he sang them Shakespearean love songs), and here he was, talking about the vote. Abraham was so impressed with the great reaction he received from his dying words that he became more alert. "He's changed his mind," his son David said. "And now he wants a glass of wine." Amidst a round of applause, Abraham got the wine and lived a few more days.

☙ *Bhagi*

Select vegetables according to season and/or your preference. Serves 6-8.

INGREDIENTS:
1 bunch scallions, chopped
1/2 tsp. Turmeric
2 cardamom pods
dash cloves
1 small piece cinnamon stick
2 tsp. Garlic, smashed
salt and pepper
2 large potatoes, cut into 1-inch cubes
1 medium eggplant, cut into 1-inch cubes
1/4 lb. (110 gm) cauliflower
1/2 lb. (225 gm) whole, small okra
1/4 lb. (110 gm) peas

METHOD:
Fry up the scallions in oil with all the spices. Add cubed potatoes, then the eggplant, then the cauliflower, giving each a little time to cook. Add any other left-over veggies. Add okra and peas at the end so that they are al dente. Cover with lid and cook on medium low until potatoes are soft. Add salt and pepper, of course. NOT ENOUGH SALT!

❧ *Gangi Chicken*

Serve with boiled rice. An easy meal for impromptu company. Serves 4.

INGREDIENTS:
2 large onions, sliced thin
1 whole chicken, cut up
Oil – canola for more crispy; olive for more yummy
1/2 tsp. turmeric
1/2 tsp. ground cumin
salt & pepper to taste
1/3 tsp. paprika
2 tsp. garlic, smashed
small handful cilantro leaves, chopped
2-3 cardamom pods

METHOD:
Preheat oven to 375°F (190°C). Lay sliced onions in roasting pan. Sprinkle chicken with garlic, spices and cilantro on both sides. Place chicken on top of onions and drizzle with oil. Put pan into oven and cook for 35-40 min; turn chicken & cook 30 min longer.

♋ *Places We Called Home*

We returned to London in 1952 on our way to America and saw our cousins from Baghdad again. My cousin May, now well settled in London, graciously took me to my first ballet performance. I felt so grown up sitting in the highest reaches at Covent Garden and was thrilled with *Giselle* danced by the Sadlers Wells company. It was different during our first journey to London in June 1946 after World War II. The war was over. In London there were large gaping holes in the streets and the rubble of bombed buildings everywhere. It was a time of shortages and everyone had ration cards for food, clothing, petrol and even soap. The weekly meat ration for our family of six was a leg of lamb. I made regular treks to the basement of Harrods for pippin apples, canned goods, jams, cheeses, butter and freshly baked bread and cakes. We were one of the fortunate. All I said was "Charge it please." Years later, after reading the *Eloise* books to my children, I realized that I had been "Eloise in London."

My parents had a good time going to clubs, gambling and attending concerts. One evening when they came home from a club, my mother came into our bedroom very excited. "We saw the princesses this evening. They looked so beautiful." "But tell them what happened," said Dad. "Well," Mum continued, "Elizabeth told Margaret that it was time to go home and Margaret replied, 'You go, I don't have a crown to look after.'" Evidently, everyone at the club found this hilarious.

My parents often went to Paris, an easy trip, to see Edith Piaf. Mum always claimed that Dad fell in love with Piaf together with half the male population of Paris. They visited Milan and were lucky enough to hear Benjamino Gigli perform at La Scala. "We met Gigli after the opera with our friends and we spoke to him," my mother remembers. "Gigli asked us where we were from and seemed quite surprised that we were from India. Then he said to me, 'Don't ever change.'"

In spite of the food shortages we ate very well. My mother, being of inventive Kurdi stock, managed to contrive delicious meals out of canned corned beef. *Ungree* was one such creation. This Arabic dish, which is usually cooked with fish (just as scarce as fresh meat back then), features fresh eggplant, tomatoes, red onions and potatoes or rice. Mum substituted corned beef for the fish and voila, good eating. She also made us *pish pash* (soup) with leftover chicken and rice for cold winter nights. *Mahmoosa*, a favorite of our family's, is made with eggs, potatoes, onions and any other fresh vegetable of your choice. Since we could buy all three main ingredients without a ration card, *mahmoosa* became a regular part of our menu. Even Dad got involved with the cooking and made the *halech* for Passover when we lived in England and America.

Luckily we were in London during the Christmas holidays and went to Pantomime, a holiday theater for children, where our first show was *Mother Goose*. On another occasion my parents took us to a show in Drury Lane. There were huge crowds in the street and a lot of yelling when we left the theater. Sir Winston Churchill was leaving one theater while Clement Attlee was leaving another. At the time they were running against each other for the position of prime minister. Attlee made a "V" for victory sign and the crowd began to scream. Then Churchill did something with one of the fingers on his right hand and the crowd went wild. I turned to my father and said, "Daddy, what is Mr. Churchill doing with his finger up in the air?" My father, who was cracking up said, "Never mind!"

My parents took us to the dog races at night as a special treat. The racing seemed absurd to me. A few greyhounds chased after a car that had a stick with some meat or other enticement hanging on it. The greyhounds I had seen on a farm where they were raised looked much more elegant than their colleagues who were running around a track in the middle of the night in London. We had excellent seats in a box overlooking the track, and now and then drinks and treats were brought to us. But the greatest treat was meeting Cary Grant in the lift. Dad and I were headed downstairs and he was the only other person in the lift. And at 13, I looked at Dad and said in a loud whisper, "Daddy, that's Cary Grant." The handsome actor smiled at me and Dad smiled back. When we got back to my family, of course our encounter was my primary topic of conversation. For the rest of the evening I ignored the dogs and kept looking around to see what other famous star was hiding in the wings.

One of the most embarrassing times of Dad's life was in London. He was taken to a posh club by important business associates who wanted to introduce him to a steam bath. Dad was delighted at the idea in the frosty winter in London, and off went three gentlemen to savor the heat and warmth. While they were in the steam bath a waiter came to the men and asked what they would like to drink. Dad's friends ordered lemonade and ginger beer. Dad said, "A pot of tea." "A pot of tea, sir?" came the reply. "Yes," said Dad. "And hot!" We laughed our heads off when he explained to us later that evening, "I kept touching the cup and the pot and they kept getting hotter and hotter. I didn't understand it at all." He got it eventually and asked for a cold soda. When I told my son Ben this story he said, "Sounds like Poppa."

My yearlong sojourn in an English boarding school was ghastly. I was the only Jewish girl in the school. England was losing both Palestine and India at that time and we were strongly connected to both. My parents were well off, as were others at the school, but they were the only parents in America and we were the only children who received large boxes of Barracini chocolates. The girls disliked me intensely as I got very good grades and was popular with the boys. After all, I wasn't British (I was), and I was a Jew! Most of the time the girls kept me in *Coventry*, a state of ostracism, and for someone from a noisy and loving family environment, that was painful. But when the chocolates arrived, I shared them with chatty girls who quickly became unfriendly once the box emptied. We went to church every Sunday and I refused to kneel. In my heritage we had been taught to never bow down in worship. From then on I had to attend the services, dressed like the other students in my uniform, but was asked to wait outside the church through the services. I felt like an "infidel" and was thrilled to go to New York in June of 1947 when the school year ended.

The first words from my lips to my parents on arrival at LaGuardia were, "If you send me back to boarding school I will throw myself from the plane." High drama for a 13 year old. Amazingly enough my brothers never felt the meanness from the boys during that year that I had felt from the girls.

New York was terrifying after the countryside of Hampshire. There were so many people and so many accents, but I could buy as much chocolate as I had ever dreamed of. Quite a contrast to postwar England. And so many exciting new experiences. As my parents were enamoured of American modern inventions we were the only household on our block that had a television set. We met Ed Sullivan, Lucy, The Honeymooners, and, most memorable of all to me, baseball. I became an ardent Brooklyn Dodgers fan who were the underdogs while the Yankees and Giants seemed to me uptown and snooty. Coney Island also had Nathan's hot dogs which, we were to realize in later years, were the best hot dogs on the planet.

Jazz Club – left to right – Dad, Aunt Rae Benjamin, Uncle Jack Benjamin, Aunt Fritz, Aunt Florrie, Uncle Joe, Mum, Uncle Jack Ezekiel

Of course it might have been because I had a huge crush on Gil Hodges, the "only gentleman" in baseball. Shortstop Pee Wee Reese, Orlando Cepeda and Jackie Robinson wound together a storybook magic that appealed to me. Manager Leo Durocher became a household name and Dad was so taken by it all that he was often home early to catch the World Series. Friends of mine and my brothers would sit on the floor, eating snacks and watching games. Abe and Ike played out on the street, using (and eventually breaking) a baseball bat given to them that was signed by Babe Ruth. None of us realized it's future value - my parents simply thought it was nice that the boys were playing outside. On my return to India, I started a team with my Maccabi friends, but our version of baseball was laughable.

My parents continued their cultural and club excursions in New York. At a performance of *Finian's Rainbow*, they sat next to Al Jolson whose songs they both loved. On Mum's 90th birthday party my brother Ike honored her with a rendition of Jolson singing "Mammy." Mum loved it.

The Cotton Club in Harlem, which was in its heyday was a favorite destination. One morning I was amazed to find Maxine Sullivan in our kitchen having breakfast. She was one of the jazz greats of the time, well known for her versions of "Loch Lomond" and "'SWonderful." My parents had brought her home after a show in Harlem to continue the party. I had to restrain myself from belting out my favorite Fats Waller song, "His Feet Too Big for De Bed." I was probably the only kid in Great Neck who even knew of Fats Waller. What a breakfast we had with Maxine Sullivan, who was delighted with *ajja*, our traditional feta cheese omelet.

To Pearl,

With Sincerest

Wishes,

Maxine Sullivan

Maxine Sullivan's autograph, probably from 1947 or 1948

෯ *Ungree*

Have a loaf of sourdough bread ready to soak up the juices. Can be prepped in advance and cooked before eating. *Faaudal*. Serves 4 to 6

INGREDIENTS:
2 large red onions
6 large tomatoes
2 medium eggplants
2 filets fish (2 lbs.)
olive oil
salt and pepper to taste
1/2 to 1 tsp. turmeric
bread crumbs

METHOD:
Preheat oven to 300°F (150°C). Slice red onions into large, flat round slices. Fry in olive oil until golden brown and place in the bottom of a deep casserole, 18"x10". Slice tomatoes into thick round slices; salt and set aside. Slice eggplant into thin round slices; set on paper towels, salt, and let drain for 1 hour. The salt will help to drain out excess water.

When eggplant is well drained, fry until browned in olive oil and set on paper towels. Peel and slice potatoes into thick slices; drizzle with salt, pepper and turmeric. Fry and brown the potatoes in olive oil and set aside.

In the casserole place the above ingredients in layers as follows:
Onions, potatoes, eggplant, fish slices, onions, tomatoes.
Cover with a second layer of ingredients.

Sprinkle the top layer of tomatoes with bread crumbs. Bake for 1 hour.

 Halech

Cooked dates used for Haroses during Passover

INGREDIENTS:
5 lbs. large pitted dates
1/4 – 1/2 tsp. anise in powdered form
1/2 lb. walnuts, chopped

METHOD:
Cook dates slowly in water, adding enough water to avoid burning. Add the anise gently while the dates are cooking.

When the dates are cooked, put them into a cuisine art and blend adding a little water as they blend to get a pulpy consistency. Serve cold with chopped walnuts for haroses.

ငဩ *Ajja*

Feta cheese omelet. A great breakfast, lunch or quick dinner, with crusty French bread or hot pita bread. Good lunch with a zesty Salade Tomate (pg. 223). A glass of Chardonnay or Fume Blanc and *bon appetit*. Serves 1.

INGREDIENTS:
2 eggs
3 oz feta cheese
butter

Stir eggs and add cheese. Mix well and fry in butter.

∞ *Mahmoosa*

Serves 4.

INGREDIENTS:
8 eggs
2 medium yellow onions, chopped
4 potatoes, peeled and cubed into 1" pieces
1 cup fresh green peas (in season) or any fast-cooking vegetable you like
salt and pepper to taste
2 cloves garlic, smashed
1 tsp. ground ginger
1/2 tsp. turmeric

METHOD:
Saute onions on medium flame in olive oil until light brown. Add garlic, ginger, turmeric and potatoes and brown. Add green peas and cook on low for 5 minutes. Stir in whisked eggs and serve when eggs are ready. Add salt & pepper to taste.

ℭ𝔰 *Pish Pash*

A recipe for colds, flu, or whatever ails you. Serves 4-6.

INGREDIENTS:
1/2 chicken, de-boned and cut into pieces
1-2 cups (227-454 gm) washed rice
1 medium yellow onion, diced
1/4 tsp. each garlic powder, ginger powder and turmeric
1 tomato, parboiled, peeled and mashed
salt & pepper to taste
1 Tbsp. olive oil

METHOD:
Gently brown onion in olive oil until golden brown. Add chicken pieces, rice and spices – brown together. Add 2 cups of water for each cup of rice. Bring to boil. Cook on simmer until rice is cooked.

Back to Bombay

Part VI

❧ *Silvercloud*

Travel by ship was my mother's favorite way to move around the globe. She took us on many illustrious ships during our childhood, starting with the troopship *Georgic*, when we sailed from Bombay to England in June 1946. The *Georgic* was packed with British soldiers returning home from the war. They slept on the decks, but there were no complaints to be heard, even in stormy weather. They were thrilled to be going home. They were quiet and, I think, in a state of exhaustion and shock. The cuisine left a lot to be desired from our point of view, but the soldiers did not seem to care.

Our next journey, from America back to India in 1948, was on a cargo ship named the *SS Hoegh Silvercloud*. We moved from a vibrant postwar America to the turmoil in India during partition. A sweet memory I have from that voyage is the exquisite taste of the tomatoes that we ate when we broke journey in Aden, on the southern tip of the Arabian Peninsula. Years later, at the airport in Martinique, I tasted *salade tomate* and thought how wonderful the tomatoes of Aden would be served that way. This was the most memorable of our sea voyages.

The P&O *SS Himalaya*, which we took from Bombay to England in 1952, was a huge contrast to our journeys on the *Georgic* and *Silvercloud*. We were in fine cabins; the food was plentiful and excellent, especially the wonderful cheeses and ice creams from New Zealand. We even had a team of Romanian gymnasts on board who practiced on the top deck.

In 1952, we took the Cunard Line's opulent *Queen Elizabeth I* from London to New York. Mum was in her element as she introduced us to the grand life. Shoshanna played in a nursery built around a Snow White and the Seven Dwarves theme. She was busy from morning till

night. Abe and Ike swam, played shuffleboard and bingo, and went
to movies; Abe even got a little drunk on the after-dinner cheeses,
which sat in large glass containers full of port. I had a glamorous
time with beautiful new dresses for dancing every night to a heavenly
band. There were plenty of single men who were delighted to squire
a 17-year-old around the dance floor. And of course, we ate the most
divine food at every meal — and at the meals between meals.

Dinner on the Q.E.

But it is the voyage on the *Silvercloud* that stands out. In 1948,
my parents moved back to India after only one year in America. My
mother was very homesick and my father wanted to reestablish his
business base in Bombay. Our parents did not discuss this latest
change with us. In a period of two years, we had attended three
different schools and lived in three distinctly different cultures on
three different continents. For me it was a numbing experience. No
sooner had I made friends and learned some of the ways in a new

country than we would move and I would lose my friends and have to start all over again. I was both sad and scared and began to wonder if I would ever have friends.

My parents decided on the *Silvercloud* because it was a Norwegian ship and Norway was politically neutral on issues between Egypt and the newly declared state of Israel. We would be passing through the Suez Canal and Jewish passengers were often detained or taken into temporary custody by the Egyptian authorities, who were hostile to Israel.

The *Silvercloud* took us from Newport News, Virginia, to Bombay in June of 1948. There were only seven passengers: Mum, myself (13), Abe (10), Ike (7), and Shoshanna (4), a young Pakistani student and an American missionary on her first journey from her home in the Midwest. Abe often was (and still is) serious and quiet. He had a wonderful time playing games, reading, doing puzzles and chatting with the crewmen. Ike was outgoing and gregarious and loved to laugh (which is most appropriate since his name, Isaac, means laughter). He was always smiling and ready for a new adventure and his happy disposition endeared him to everyone on board. My brothers spent a lot of time together having fun, and whenever we came to a port their level of excitement reached a crescendo. Shoshanna was a beautiful little doll who asked a lot of questions. Her curiosity propelled her all about the ship keeping my mother quite active. In my memory, my mother looked like a movie star. She was in her mid-thirties, charming and practical and with a flair and style all her own.

The ship was spotless, the crew constantly washing, repainting and refurbishing different areas. Each of the crew looked "spick and span" with clean clothes, Nordic blond hair and tall bodies with cheerful blue eyes that seemed to look at the world unabashed. The person I remember best was the chief operating officer, an uncharacteristically dark-haired, dark eyed Norwegian in his 40s who watched over us carefully during our journey through the Suez Canal. He took me to the bridge many times to show me how the ship operated and even gave me the wheel to steer, making me feel important as if he sensed my complete state of loneliness.

I also remember well the young Pakistani student, who read a lot and was quiet; it was rumored that he had nothing but books in his many boxes of luggage. He had just graduated from Harvard but was not too proud to play cards or chess with Abe and me. My cabin mate was the American missionary. She was so shy, I can't remember having had a conversation with her. We scarcely saw her between meals, and although she was only in her late 20s she seemed old in her timidity.

Ike was constantly attempting feats of daring. Back when he was about two, he would jump off my parent's cupboards into the arms of one of their card-playing friends. Everyone would laugh and he would be rewarded with a few rupees. In the middle of the Atlantic Ocean, this seven-year-old jumped from an upper deck of the ship to the deck below. His goal, which he accomplished, was to land in the lifeboat tied onto the lower deck. He probably didn't understand why everyone was so upset. He remembered being rewarded for this type of behavior before. Why the anger instead of "Great job" and "Here's your reward"? (Ike says he knew the sailors could see him and he remembers the stunt as a lark.)

The chief operating officer was not amused. He took Ike into the captain's quarters and spanked him. It was the first time I had ever seen a grown man with tears in his eyes, with a bawling Ike in tow. Ike had touched a chord in him and it was evident that spanking Ike hurt him deeply.

In fact, Ike may have been inspired by events at sea. Before his wild jump we had seen magnificent schools of porpoise leaping through the waves. They looked like they were having a great time and seemed to be aware of their audience. In all my sea voyages, I have never felt as in awe as I did watching those porpoises fly through the air and hearing them making sounds that seemed to say, "Watch me, Ma."

After that adventure the rest of the journey was uneventful. Blue skies and more blue seas. Schools of dolphins and even, on one occasion, an albatross. The constancy of the sea and sky became wearisome. If we saw another ship it was an occasion to cheer and made me feel reconnected with the world.

Even more wearisome was the food, which was dull and boring and tasted like the boarding school fare I had endured in England and India, where the cooks prepared gristly meats for their captives. On the *Silvercloud*, the so-called curries and dahl were watery and insipid and even the rice stuck together in indigestible chunks. Canned peaches were served for every dessert (to this day I can't stand canned peaches). I soon learned the favorite seaman's diet of melba toast, or any hard toast and salted dried meats. By the time we arrived in Bombay after 28 days at sea, I had lost 28 pounds. Now *that's* a diet!

The weather could be equally disagreeable. At one point we hit a huge storm in the Mediterranean and were ordered below deck for two days. My childish daring, however, took me to the top deck one day and I had to cling to the door on my knees. I could only get back below deck by crawling down the stairs. The waves were so high I could have been tossed over in a jiffy. (Out of panic, I slept in my mother's cabin with my sister and brothers during this storm.) Cooped up in our bunks, we amused ourselves by racing oranges marked with little flags across the floor. We sang school songs from our various schools and spent the rest of the time reading, sleeping early, and getting up late.

By the time we reached Egypt the seas had quieted. But the calm was deceptive. As we glided into Port Said to go through the canal at 2:30 in the morning, all five of us were woken up and, in a semi stupor, brought to the captain's cabin by some of the crew. We found our burly, bearded captain having a heated argument with an Egyptian official who wanted to remove our entire family from the ship. The official demanded our passports and stamped them "J." The captain was furious, banging his fist on his desk and repeating, in a red-faced roar, "Norway is neutral! These are my passengers!" But the Egyptian official insisted that we could be Israeli spies.

Finally he gave in, all the while protesting that this mother and her four children were "the enemy." We were members of the militant Irgun, he felt sure, and would each require an Egyptian soldier to guard us. Later that morning Abe was taking photos of the port with his Brownie camera when a soldier came up to him, grabbed the camera, pulled out the film and threw it in the water. Abe was quiet and showed no anger or emotion, while I, with my transparent nature, glared at the soldier.

Our guards were poor men who had probably joined King Farouk's small riffraff army for money and food. Their clothes were in tatters. Their shoes were old and they were all very thin with hungry eyes. But each one had a gun with a bayonet slung over his shoulder at all times. The five days and nights through the canal became an ordeal. I dressed behind the cupboard door when I realized a soldier was leering at me through the deck porthole of my cabin. I faced each day with dread. Normally talkative, I became silent. The silence penetrated the ship as sharp and bright as the edge of the knives on the guns around us. For months after we arrived in Bombay, I slept far away from the window in our bedroom and never left the house alone. I kept thinking there was someone following me to kill me. It made me wonder how prisoners in concentration camps ever managed to survive after living in their constant state of terror.

Our shipmates were also affected by our experience. The American missionary was shocked by our treatment. And it was difficult not to notice the quiet fury and frustration of the captain, the chief officer and of Mr. Khan, the Pakistani student, who was particularly enraged that his fellow Muslims could treat a harmless woman and her four small children in this manner.

Ike probably suffered the most. All of seven, he was having a hard time controlling his bladder in the midst of our new gun-toting companions. In spite of his outward cheerful demeanor, Ike's body had taken over. He was embarrassed and quiet. My mother called a meeting of the captain, the chief officer, Mr. Khan and me. She wanted a couple of the guards to take Ike off the ship and let him have some fun. That, she was sure, would help him overcome his fear. She knew the Arab spirit better than any of us, she said, and she thought her plan was a good one.

The four of us were dumbfounded. We looked at one another, and then at her, in dismay. There was no question in our minds that Ike would never return to the ship alive. But as the five of us sat at a round table in the captain's cabin my mother was insistent. The captain became curt and said that Norway would not accept responsibility for her action. I looked imploringly at the men whose body language reflected my feelings that this idea of my mother's was mad. "You are killing my brother!" I said, a lot for an obedient daughter from my strict Indian/Iraqi background, but the men in the room had given me the courage to speak out.

In the end she got her way and Ike took off with two of the guards and plenty of dollars in their pockets. It was like the story of the sacrificed Isaac. In my mind, my mother was letting my brother die;

my brother, whom I adored and who meant so much to me. And there were three worldly grown-ups who agreed with me. My fury was laced with mourning. I hated her for getting her way and taking a chance with Isaac's life.

For what seemed an eternity, Mr. Khan, the captain, the chief officer, and I walked around the ship in a daze. I could not look at my mother or speak to her. She carried on as if nothing out of the ordinary were taking place and moved through the day in a manner that seemed to say, "I know what I'm doing." With her tradition steeped in the Middle East and her fluency in Arabic, my mother behaved as if she had a strategy. She had been quietly talking to our guards in their dialect and had told them stories of her ties to the Smouha family of Alexandria. The Smouhas were an old philanthropic Jewish family who had helped poor people for generations. The guards knew of them and were impressed with my mother's connection to Egyptian Jews they held in high esteem. My mother enhanced her position with generous *baksheesh* (bribes).

Ike returned after five hours further down the canal, carrying balloons, sweets and small toys. He and the compliant guards were all smiles and one can only imagine how much *baksheesh* exchanged hands that day. He remained unafraid for the rest of the journey.

At Suez our guards left the ship, along with the women who had boarded the ship in Port Said and then disappeared below deck for the entire journey. The same Egyptian official showed up on the dock and stared at us as if he still wanted to throw us all overboard. Within minutes of his appearance, my mother spewed out her entire Arabic vocabulary of curses on him, his family and his people. He was visibly shocked.

Our next port of call was Karachi, Pakistan, where Mr. Khan, who we realized was a minister in Pakistan, came to the ship to greet his son. When he heard about our episodes in the canal, Mr. Khan invited us all home for tea. My mother, again observing cultural tradition, refused, as she said she could not break bread with a Muslim after what had happened to her and her children. But she suggested that she would accept an escort to take us to the famous Karachi Zoo for an outing while the ship was loading and unloading cargo. Before we knew it a long black limousine flying the flag of Pakistan pulled up and took us to the zoo, where we rode around on the backs of our own elephants, in high style. I loved visiting a zoo this way, perched on an amazing creature looking at other amazing creatures. The Khans tried to make up for our difficulties and were very sad and embarrassed by the behavior of their Muslim brothers.

Ironically, in the late 1980s, my brother Abraham, of the famous Brownie camera, helped negotiate a settlement between Egypt and Israel in his capacity as legal counsel for the State Department. The region in dispute was Taba and it took five years of negotiation to arrive at a resolution whereby Israel returned Taba to Egypt and Egypt's ambassador returned to Israel.

Eventually I was able to put aside the fears I had experienced to focus on the rest of our journey. I remember the sounds of greedy, shrieking beggar gulls whose cries were matched by the young boys in small boats hawking their wares. I came to love the memories of the sweet sounds of the *fellaheen* (tillers of the soil) singing and playing drums and flutes after dusk, as if they were welcoming the night. Their melodies were reassuring and lulled me to sleep. There is an exquisite peace in the desert when night falls. All creatures lie down together and seem to join the ancient Pharaohs in their rest. The journey made me fantasize images of Egyptian princesses on small boats taking a leisurely journey on the water. All those sounds and memories have stayed with me much longer than the fears.

෬ *Salade Tomate*

This salad has become a standard part of my diet. Serves 4.

INGREDIENTS:
2 large beefsteak tomatoes, sliced
salt and pepper to taste
lemon juice or balsamic vinegar to taste
olive oil

METHOD:
Lay tomatoes on a flat serving plate. Sprinkle with olive oil, salt, pepper and lemon juice or balsamic vinegar to taste.

☙ After Partition

We arrived back in Bombay amid the turmoil of partition between the Hindus and Muslims. Mahatma Gandhi had finally won India back for her people from the British, but the map of India that he inherited highlighted the divisions between "Hindu India" and "Muslim Pakistan." This division led to unrest and religious uprisings for territory and power. India still has the second-largest Muslim population (after Indonesia) in the world. When I visited Hyderabad I saw Hindus and Muslims living together in peace and still wonder how the politics of this large country would have been if it had not been broken up into separate countries. Would it have been more peaceful without the continual conflict over Kashmir and the polarization of religious factions? As a Jew I always have felt that India is a unique and peaceful homeland to a variety of religious beliefs.

But back to partition. The British imposed a curfew that began at 6 p.m. to control the riots that flared between Hindus and Muslims. From my window I saw two British soldiers with a machine gun at our street corner for many nights. Imagine, given the heat of India, having to be indoors by 6 p.m. I wondered where the people who normally slept on the streets went. One day as I came home from school I saw an open-bed truck piled with bodies heading to the ocean to be dumped. I remember feeling that my throat had stuck in my chest. I wanted to throw up but couldn't. It is estimated that a million people were killed during partition and seventy-five thousand women were abducted and raped.

It was a gory period of history that culminated in the untimely murder of Gandhi by one of his own people because he had spoken kindly with Muslims while on a visit to Calcutta. My cousin Effry tells me how frightening it was in Calcutta: "There were riots in India where the Hindus and the Muslims slaughtered one another. And in Bengal it was called 'The Great Killing of Calcutta.' But, you know, other people, the Jews and the Parsis {refugee Zoroastrians, a religious group from Persia who made India their home}, were not interfered with. And because of his position, my father was given a gun and he always had guards walking with him wherever he went." In Bombay, both the Hindus and Muslims would often warn the Jews when there would be trouble and both would separately share rumors that "the British had ordered a riot."

Despite the violence associated with partition, we were back in Firuz Ara surrounded by our aunts, uncles, grandparents and a multitude of cousins and friends. Unlike the nomadic existence of the last few years, my life back in Bombay meant that I never had to worry about making new friends and then losing them. My cousins, by themselves, created a forest of friends.

Our Bombay gang

I resumed all my favorite sports activities, from dressage at 6 a.m. before school, to swimming, badminton, table tennis, field hockey, netball, tennis and cycling. It was a whirl of parties where we practiced the latest Western dances together with the hora and other Israeli folk dances. We went to Juhu Beach in overcrowded cars usually borrowed from older family members. No one had a car. And if we had enough money, we went to the Sun n' Sand Hotel for soft drinks feeling like *burra sahibs* (big shots). From time to time we rented bicycles to go up and down Malabar Hill. Lots of movies, family celebrations and fun, fun, fun. I never wanted to leave India again.

Not only was my own life a joy, but my parents also had an active social life. They had friends and family around them. They went to the Jewish Club to play cards a few nights a week and Dad was one of their top-notch billiard players. He allowed Abe, Ike and me to watch him play during a tournament if we kept totally quiet; Ike eventually left the room but Abe and I remained to see our dad win the cup. Almost every Saturday night my parents went to the Taj Mahal Hotel to dance. They loved to dance and they loved the latest in American jazz. Horse races every weekend and dinners at good restaurants rounded out their full social schedule.

Mum, Dad, and Aunts Soph and Iris with friends at the Taj

Meanwhile our commitment to Israel and *habra* (charity) never stopped. I felt the thrill of the freedom of both India and Israel and was emotionally dedicated to both. I sang "Hindustan Hamara Hai" (India Is Mine) and the "Hatikvah." The pain of India was my pain.

Nearly 300 years of British rule had divided and denuded the land. At the Tower of London I felt deep anger when I saw the showcases of Indian gems displayed as part of British wealth. Even the Kohinoor diamond was grandly exhibited in London and claims were made that inferred it was a gift to Britain by the people of India.

In Bombay we did what we could to raise funds for Israel and I had the good fortune to attend a concert starring Yehudi Menuhin in 1950 when he played at the Cowasji Jehangir Hall in Bombay. He had come to encourage the people of India, and the Jewish community in particular, to support Israel. He played with Ravi Shankar and this amazing experience was my first, very personal introduction to the blending of fine classical Indian and European music. Many years later I had the pleasure to hear them perform together again in San Francisco. As good, if not better.

After the concert there was a dinner party at the home of the first Israeli ambassador to India and his wife. All the important Jewish people in the community were there and it must have been considered a very special event because my mother personally prepared and supervised the cooking of over 200 *arook*, the delicious fried Iraqi rice balls stuffed with ground breast of chicken with spices. *Arook* is seldom, if ever, seen on menus as it is labor intensive. But it's well worth it for a very special event and brought in more shekels for Israel at that dinner.

Now, as an adult, I realize the significance of my family's multicultural experiences in India. Our close friends included Hindus, Muslims, Catholics, Parsis, Jews, British, Chinese, and Americans, and our friendships with them, I feel, have given my siblings and me a continued global viewpoint. We lived in what used to be considered a third world, ruled by the British Raj, then moved to postwar England, and touched down briefly in America.

The variety of schools we attended began with a Dominican Convent for me and the Anglican Cathedral for my brothers in Bombay. Then there were boarding schools in Poona and Panchgani. My big surprise at Kimmins, the boarding school in Panchgani, was the signs pointing to "Fairyland." This turned out to be the special name for "bathroom," which was considered indelicate at a school for young British ladies. In England we attended a Church of England boarding school where I first heard the word *kike*. The following year, in America, we went to public schools in Great Neck, New York, and when we returned to India we attended an American missionary school called Woodstock.

Woodstock was located in Mussourie in the foothills of the Himalayas, over 6,000 feet above sea level. We could see the mountains in our back yard, and when the sun set in October, every student was on the veranda watching in total silence and awe. I have never seen anything so beautiful anywhere before or since. We were in wild country but I never believed it until one evening after a meeting at the principal's home. We were rehearsing a play that I had written and was directing. Rehearsal was over, it was late, and we were leaving the house to head to our dorms. Suddenly we heard our principal's Alsatian barking furiously and noticed a low hissing and growling. We went outside and saw a crouching black panther, ready to jump the dog. The two animals attacked each other and we watched, horrified but unable to look away. The principal moved us closer to the front door and went inside. He came out with his gun and shot both the panther and the dog.

At Kimmins, the boarding school I was sent to in Panchgani, I experienced one of my most special times with my father. My mother explained to me years later that many Jewish girls in Bombay were sent to Kimmins because Japanese submarines had been sighted in the bay of Bombay. The horror stories that came to us across the seas about the abuse of girls in China by the Japanese motivated many mothers to send their young daughters far away from Bombay. My father surprised me one weekend by showing up at Kimmins and taking me to a lovely old boarding house for two days. He was accompanied by Aunt Rae and her husband, Uncle Jack. Aunt Rae introduced me to the delight of picking fresh tomatoes off a bush and eating them. Dad took me for *gaary* rides where he taught me the songs "I've Got Sixpence" and "Nice People with Nice Manners but Got No Money at All." The grim year at Kimmins was swept away by the memories of having the undivided attention of my father for that weekend. I felt like a princess. I realized that boarding schools were not my cup of tea. I ended up at Walsingham House School in Bombay, where I graduated the Senior Cambridge exams with top honors.

I am forever indebted to my motherland, India, for the freedom and hospitality that she extended to the Jews of Iraq. The one-time Jewish community of over 150,000, including the Cochin and Bene Israel Jews, has shrunk to a few thousand. The Jews of India scattered to America, Australia, Canada, England and Israel after independence as most businesses were taken over by Indian enterprises. But the synagogues, schools, library and graveyards remain. Most, if not all of these symbols of our time in India, were supported by the financial backbone of our community, the Sassoon family of Baghdad, who eventually became members of British royalty.

The exposure to different traditions has helped all of us in our various professions. Abe's work as an international mediator benefited from his early understanding of a variety of global issues; Ike developed a depth of understanding for the suffering that human beings experienced and has applied this knowledge as a therapist; Shoshanna has used what she has seen in India and America to humanize the public health arena; and my work has encompassed mediation between families from diverse backgrounds in conflict resolution. We have been able to work with people from all walks of life and from many countries as a result of growing up in Bombay and in other countries of our world.

 *Arook*

With a zesty salad, this recipe should serve 4 happy people.

INGREDIENTS:
2 cups cooked basmati rice, mashed
I egg
2 cups chopped chicken breasts
I cup coarse bread crumbs (not fine)
1/4 tsp. garlic salt, pepper, cumin and turmeric.
2 Tbsp. chopped cilantro or parsley

METHOD:
Cook rice and cool.

Beat egg and add, a little at a time to the rice until consistency is okay for molding into 2" to 3" diameter balls. Put in refrigerator while you cook the chicken.

Fry chopped chicken in olive oil with spices until browned. Cool in refrigerator.

Take rice balls and with your thumb form a hole in each ball. Stuff with enough chicken mixture to fill the rice ball without falling out of the rice. Fold the rice back into a ball with the chicken inside Roll onto bread crumbs and brush lightly with olive oil. In a 3" to 4" deep frying pan brown a thin layer of olive oil. Fry the arook, turning each one carefully, using two plastic spoons. Cook until browned, at least 20 min. Drain on paper towels and serve.

೧೫ *Hide and Seek*

We left Bombay in 1952 after the father of my brother Ike's friend Kumar, was murdered. Kumar, Ike and their friend Jack were playing hide and seek at Kumar's home, right around the corner from Firuz Ara. I remember the terrible screaming when Ike returned home that afternoon and fell into my mother's arms. He was trembling, gesticulated with his arms and couldn't speak. We had never seen him so scared and out of control. None of us knew what had happened until the servants came running into the flat with a variety of stories about the "dead man." Murders never happened in Bombay during my childhood, and it was terrifying to find out that Ike was a part of this sad episode.

One afternoon on his backyard deck in Oakland, Ike told me what he remembered:

> "I was playing hide and seek with my friends Kumar and Jack outside the building. I was hidden around the corner from the front entrance of the house when Kumar's dad walked in and then another man followed him into the building. Suddenly I heard a lot of shouting and saw the man who had gone into the house after Kumar's dad run out with a long, blood-soaked knife in his hands. That man never saw me and raced into the street waving his knife. A policeman was coming down the street, and when they saw one another, the killer challenged the unarmed policeman with his knife. The policeman backed off and the killer ran away. Kumar and Jack saw the killer waving his knife at the policeman and so did other people on the street. Kumar's father meanwhile had been taken upstairs to his flat, and I followed my friend to his house. People were crying and many of the women were screaming. I was very shook up and after a while I ran home."

"I always felt like the middle child," Ike said. Invisible in his home and in deep need of attention, he was the second son, his brother Abe the coveted first. Shoshanna was the baby of the family. I was the eldest. Ike felt that he had no position in the order of siblings. In Kumar's home, he felt needed and decided he would do anything he could to help his friend. "I felt that I had to take care of Kumar and his mother." He was just nine years old and very vulnerable in spite of an outward show of bravado. When the English detective fed him a story of what he had seen, Ike readily agreed with the detective's version that he had been an eyewitness, a total fabrication. Since everyone on the street saw the killer run out of the building, covered in blood and carrying a bloodied knife, there was no real need for an eyewitness, of course. "In retrospect, I feel I was used and set up by the detective," Ike said. "I made it easier for him to win the case and that's all the detective wanted."

The three boys were taken to a lineup at the jail after the killer was caught and they readily identified him. The killer's family lived within a mile of our flat and they threatened to kill Ike. Police were posted outside our building and a guard was assigned to Ike, even at school. The policeman became Ike's shadow wherever he went in Bombay. All this terrified him even more. He told me he had a very difficult time going to sleep at night, imagining that the killer was coming into his room to knife him. "I waited, every day, to be killed." He would eventually go to sleep and dream that he was being stabbed like his friend's father.

We left Bombay as soon as we could after that with the police guards still around us. My mother was anxious all the time and urgently felt the need to leave. There is no telling how many more years we would have remained in our idyllic paradise in Bombay if Ike hadn't been playing hide and seek that day. It's not surprising that he is now in the business of helping people to heal their traumas and is one of the best in his field.

Appendices

❧ *List of Recipes*

In our home we used a variety of spices that can be adapted to suit your palate.

If you don't like cilantro, substitute parsley. If cumin and chilies are too hot, try paprika with more ginger and garlic. Play with the spices and always brown them in a little olive oil before using. In most Indian and Middle Eastern recipes, start with finely chopped onions, garlic, salt, pepper, and some turmeric browned in oil, commonly mustard oil for Indian food and olive oil for Middle Eastern. (My preference is olive oil as mustard oil is too strong for me.) In some recipes using chicken, we often do not use oil but let the chicken cook in its own fat after removing some of the skin.

Always use fresh parboiled and skinned tomatoes. They produce a better final flavor. Another tip: find a smooth rock that you like. Use it to "smash" garlic pods. The garlic will come out of its skin and be easier to cut and peel. Try it   it feels good.

Always wash and strain rice before cooking. The rice is cleaner and cooks faster.

Wash and strain dahl lentils several times to remove white scum on top of the water.

Soak lentils for at least one hour before using.

Servings in all recipes are approximate.

In kosher homes, substitute margarine for butter for all *samosas* and *sambusaks*.

⊂℥ *Hindi Terms*

Indian Herbs

Coriander leaves . . . . *Hara dhania*
or *kothmir*
Basil . . . . *Tulsi*
Bay leaves . . . . *Tej patta*
Mint leaves . . . . *Pudina*
Curry leaves *Curry patta* or *mitha neem*
Fenugreek leaves . . . .*Hari methi*
Garlic . . . .*Lasum*
Fresh ginger . . . . *Adrak*

Spices

Aniseeds or fennel seeds . . . . . *Saunf*
Asafoetida . . . . *Hing*
Curum . . . . *Ajwain*
Black pepper . . . . *Kali mirchi*
Cardamom . . . . *Chotee illaichi*
Black cardamom . . . . *Kali illaichi*
(not to be eaten raw)
Cloves . . . . *Lavang*
Coriander seeds . . . . . . *Sookha dhania*
Cumin seeds . . . .*Zeera*

White cumin . . . . *Safed zeera*
Black cumin . . . . *Shah zeera*
Fenugreek . . . . *Methi dana*
Mango powder . . . .*Aamchur*
Poppy seeds . . . . *Khus-khus*
Saffron . . . .*Zaffran* or *kesar*
Sesame seeds . . . . *Gingelly* or *til*
Turmeric . . . . *Haldi*
Nutmeg . . . . *Jaiphal*
Black salt or rock salt . . . *Kala namak*

Vegetables

Aubergine or Eggplant . . . . . *Baingan*
Cauliflower . . . . *Phulgobi*
Green peas . . . . *Mutter*
Okra or Ladyfinger . . . .*Bhindi*
Potato . . . .*Alu*
Beetroot . . . . *Chukander*
Onion . . . . *Piaz*
Spinach . . . .*Palak*
Carrot . . . . *Gaajar*
Lettuce . . . . *Salad ka patta*
Fenugreek leaves . . . . . . *Methi ka saag*